Do two Rons make a Knight?
–Men of Sussex–

1916 to 2000

1. December 30, 1916

Our story begins on December 30, 1916. – Ronald Pelham Knight was born in Georgian England at the height of the British Empire's colonial might. George V, grandson of Queen Victoria was King. Queen Victoria was the second British monarch of the House of Saxe-Coburg and Gotha, which as a result of anti-German sentiment would a year later change its name to The House of Windsor. It is this House that reigns today through Queen Elizabeth ll, now over sixty-years into her glorious tenure.

This was the British Empire at its apex; the largest and greatest empire the world has ever known. Starting, some would agree, in 1497 with the colonization of Newfoundland and ending five hundred years later in 1997 with the withdrawal from Hong Kong. The pace of life in rural England was slow to moderate at best. The horse was still a significant mode of transportation, both saddle and trap. The class system was comfortably in place, and each knew theirs. Few people travelled much farther than the confines of their townships and villages. This is the main reason that there are so many active accents in Britain surviving to this day. People living within fifty miles of each other would have distinctly different and distinguishable dialects comprising of words sounds and colloquialisms, and since one village rarely had need to communicate with another, the accents persisted with neither contamination nor homogenization. Even as late as the 1960s there were folk in the village of Cuckfield who had never seen the sea at the Edwardian, channel-resort of Brighton, a mere fourteen miles to the south.

Brighton is directly south of London and was popularized by the likes of the flamboyantly fashionable Beau Brummell and the then Prince of Wales, latter to become King George IV. The London to Brighton stagecoach would spend a night in The Kings Head in the small market town of Cuckfield.

2. THE GREAT WAR – WW1

1916 was slap dab in the middle of the First World War known both as the 'Great War' and the ever so optimistic 'The war to end all wars'. The chain of treaty-dictated events following the assassination in Sarajevo of Archduke Ferdinand, heir to the Austro-Hungarian throne that precipitated this war would be laughable if the results were not so catastrophic in their immense loss of life. Sixteen million dead. The insanity of this warfare is incomprehensible. The generals sitting for the most part in comfort and luxury, sent out wave after wave, each comprised of thousands of men, from trenches to attack the other side who were 'dug-in' in muddy, rat infested trenches of their own. In some cases, battles fought over a few hundred yards of meaningless sod went on for months, even years. To get some idea of the scope of destruction, do some research on the Battle of the Somme and of Passchendaele. There are a couple of movies also worth seeing: one called *Passiondale* and the other that comes to mind is *The War Horse*. And from the German perspective try *All quiet on the Western Front*.

The Great War had considerable influence on the fabric of the English establishment, and that of the rest of Europe for that matter. The young men that did manage to return to their countries were not the same as the boys that had left. They had seen, done, and experienced things, good and awful, that they never would have in their entire normal lives. That Genie was now out of the bottle and would never be put back in.

Even those that did not actually go to war were caught up with the war effort back home, changing their lives forever. Lines dividing social strata that had developed over hundreds of years from the feudal system had been crossed like never before and once crossed would never be the same. In some cases the gentry had actually worked perhaps for the first time in their lives, sometimes doing menial tasks in hospitals and in transportation. They had gone without many of the luxuries and privileges of birthright to which they had been accustomed for many generations. Things like lots of servants, exotic wines and foods, vacations, extravagant parties and so on. They were now forced to make do with less.

For the average Joe, he had fought side by side in the muck and bullets with the hoi polloi and realized that these people could fear, bleed, and die just as he could. The result was the beginning of a breakdown of what had been a simple, two-class system. Out of this emerged for the first time in England a middle class, leaving in its wake an ever so slightly less bowed and better-educated working-class, eager listeners to the philosophical teachings of Carl Marx, while the aristocracy shook more than a little in their comfortable beds in the aftermath of the Russian Revolution.

England had to change or rather continue the change that had been set in motion by the war, or it would share the fate of Russia and even that of France only one hundred years earlier. I believe that Britain rose to this challenge. It reinvented itself as indeed it had several times in its history, from the Monarchy through the composition of its parliament and society at large.

3. THE EASTER UPRISING.

It was also in 1916 that the Irish rebellion known as the Easter Uprising took place. An Irish nationalist by the name of Sir Roger Casement tried unsuccessfully to form a strong populist militia force allied to the German Kaiser that would sweep British rule from Ireland. The force turned out to be a mere one thousand men. Marching on Dublin, they occupied the main Post Office. Their hope was that all of Southern Ireland would raise up to support them. This never happened, and it is quite possible that this incident would have died a natural uninspiring death if it were not for the heavy-handed over-reaction by the British Government. They sent in a gunboat backed by five thousand troops. They shelled the city and by the time it was over, two hundred and twenty civilians had been killed, creating martyrs to the cause and giving birth to the Irish Republican Army (IRA). The country that once had knighted him, hanged Sir Roger Casement.

In my tardiness, I have not managed to understand the history of Ireland and would be silly to pretend otherwise. I read *Trinity* by Leon Uris years ago and several novels and accounts since, but that is about it. From what I have gleaned, this is my, I am sure over simplified take on it.

4. AFTER THE ROMANS: ANGLES & SAXONS.

When the Romans departed Britain around the year 400AD, they left behind a semblance of legal and social order, amazing roads, buildings, and baths. They also left a well-managed farming system. Unfortunately they left all of this unprotected. Through four centuries of occupation, the people of Britain had neither need nor option of having an army. When the Romans left, the scavengers moved in. Angles and Saxons from the part of north eastern Europe that is now Germany and Denmark, came by the hundreds of thousands – First to plunder, and then to settle. Over the next two hundred and fifty years, the Anglo-Saxons virtually wiped out the male population of Britain and drove what was left into the hills to the West and North taking with them the last semblances of the Romans' religion. The religion survived. Roman Catholic monks and priests administered to their flocks in these remote outposts of what are now Wales, Ireland, and Scotland. Though headhunted, tortured and killed, those that survived steadfastly continued their prayer and worship. They copied and transcribed volumes and volumes of holy books. The survival of those works is largely responsible for preserving the Christian faith and perhaps, civilized knowledge and learning over this period in history know as the Dark Ages. A Monk in Northumbria, referred to as the Venerable Bede, even wrote the first history of the English people. Christianity had faired a lot better across the English Channel in the land of the Franks, and holy men the likes of Augustine from Scotland and England, and Patrick from Ireland, made pilgrimages through France and on to the Holy Land and kept in touch with the Church of Rome, passing their knowledge and teachings down through their disciples.

The Anglo-Saxon raiders brought their Germanic language to Britain, and named this country the 'Land of the Angle's' from which we get the word England. Through this period there developed significant territories within England: Northumbria, Mercer, Sussex, Essex, and Wessex, which by the mid 800s had boiled down to the two dominant fiefdoms of Mercer and Wessex. These two may have continued to go at it if it were not for a new and common threat from across the North Sea.

5. THE VIKINGS.

The Vikings - mostly form Norway and Denmark attacked all along the Saxon Shores and occupied a great portion of southeast England including the city that would become London. From there, they pushed West and North destroying everything and anyone in their path. They were the ultimate consumers. They neither built nor sowed, and when they ran out of plunder, they looked to new sources. They fought various tribes as they went but perhaps the most organized resistance was to come from Alfred of Wessex.

Significant for its generous climate and arable land, was an area in the southwest called Wessex ruled by King Alfred, a Saxon Christian. He championed the church in Britain that had been revived by one of his ancestors; Aethelberht when he married a Christian princess from France called Bertha. Alfred is today considered one of the great English monarchs.

This is the Alfred that in legend 'burned the cakes'. After being severely routed in a battle with the Danes, he disguised himself as a simple soldier and took refuge among the marsh people in his western province. Alfred was never a physically strong man and suffered most of his life with extreme stomach problems so to earn his keep he was put to work in the kitchens. Unfortunately, Alfred was a thinker not a baker so, according to lore, he just watched, contemplating his future, while the cakes burned.

By sheer strength of his intellect however, Alfred the Great, would return to power claiming both his throne and place in history. He is credited as being the first to unite the provinces of Britain under one banner, ultimately driving out the Danes, and attempting to establish 'Common Law' a unique decree that gave every man the right to seek justice regardless of their social stature. This was a monumental change in culture from a system where the average person had absolutely no rights in law. He built a series of fortified towns and had a standing, mobile army. He also built a navy.

The church thrived and through wielding fear of the unknown afterlife like an ecclesiastic mace, gained in power and wealth eventually owning vast tracts of land and even employing its own armies to 'defend the faith'. It even survived the brief period of

Danish resurgent rule between 1016 and 1042 under King Canute, the same arrogant ass that placed a throne on the beach at a town called Bosham in what is now the county of Hampshire, and demanded the tide recede. He damn near drowned

There followed a brief period of restored Anglo-Saxon rule but this was wiped out by William the Conqueror in 1066. William, Duke of Normandy, a decedent of Norsemen, had been one of three contenders, all of whom had some legitimate claim to the throne vacated when Edward the Confessor, who died in January 1066 leaving no direct heirs. The throne had been grabbed by Harold Godwinson but was contested by both William and a Danish king in northern England by the name of Harold Hedrada. Godwinson had just defeated Hedrada at the battle of Stanford Bridge, when he received word that the Norman army was sighted in the English Channel. Harold force-marched his army all the way down from Yorkshire in just three days to face William at Hastings. An amazing feat in itself.

6. THE BATTLE OF HASTINGS 1066

Was it huge tactical error - Cavalry - or just bad luck?

If you ever get the chance to go to the small town of Battle, which is where the famous event took place, set aside an hour and take in the exhibition.

History describes the Saxons as holding the high ground, so the gentle slope that greeted me was a surprise. Harold had archers of course, the deadly artillery of the day, and I suppose that slope was just enough to give them an advantage.

After repelling several attacks over two days, for some historically argued reason, the Saxons broke their entrenched ranks and pursued what seemed like a routed enemy.

One of the earth shattering inventions that should share a place in history along with the wheel, is the stirrup. This simple addition to a saddle developed by the Francs in Europe, turned the horse into a mobile platform from which a warrior could fight.

The Normans had Cavalry. The concept of a fighting force using horses as strategic weapons and not just for transportation was totally unheard of in Britain at this time. As the Saxons charged down the slope on foot, Norman horsemen attacked them from both sides. They were butchered.

The Normans once again firmly established the Catholic Church in England. They consolidated the kingdom laying claim to and conquering Wales, Scotland and Ireland. Over the next three hundred years or so, England maintained claim to territories in mainland Europe, from Brittany down through Normandy to the Aquitaine in what is now part of France and along the way, fought a war with the Francs that lasted over hundred years.

Unlike the Vikings who left little to show for their two hundred years of marauding and occupation other then a lot of fair-haired children, the Normans built an incredible heritage in just about the same length of time. They ruled by merciless force but never the less, rule they did.

Recognizing the advantages to be had by association with the power of the Church of Rome, they built magnificent churches and cathedrals throughout the land. And where as the Saxons had built fortified towns to protect the population, the Normans built Castles to control them.

This was the beginning of the British class system or Feudalism. Perhaps an over simplification and with the amount of travel and cross breeding today probably inapplicable but, the common Englishman is a descendent of the Saxons while the upper-class or ruling-class are descendants of the Normans – two separate races?

7. REFORMATION. IRELAND OCCUPIED.

Catholicism continued to prosper in England in spite of the European Reformation that was taking place in France, Germany, even in Scotland, fostered by dissident churchmen such as Martin Luther and John Calvin. These men rebelled against the doctrines of the Roman church, its rituals, excesses, and structures. England with its fragile alliance with Spain remained Catholic right up to and under the Tudors until Henry VIII fell out with the Pope over not being able to have his marriage to Katherine of Aragon annulled so he could marry Anne Boleyn. In 1534, Henry broke away from Rome and established The Church of England, a Protestant Christian religion, making himself the Head of the Church and Defender of the Faith. Thus, we ended up having a Protestant England and Scotland but with a Catholic Ireland at its back.

Given the power and animosity of these two religious entities across Europe at this time, it is no wonder that the situation bred fear, hatred, and paranoia among the English rulers. For their now archenemy Spain, to have a welcome mat at the back door of England was untenable to its sovereignty and security. (The same situation would be replicated four decades later, with Germany as the protagonist.)

To meet this threat England embarked on a brutal colonization plan in which it gave land, land that it did not in truth own, to English nobles and barons in return for their keeping the local population 'in check'. (England would develop a habit of doing this sort of thing – read up on the origins of Pakistan and Israel.)

The degree to which the Irish were brutalized varied somewhat depending on the individual property owner at the time but none were pleasant. Perhaps the worst period and therefore the most notably hated were the Cromwell years of the 1650s in which his puritanical zeal was unequalled. He attacked and defeated the Royalist supporters of the Scots Stewarts who had allied themselves with the Irish Confederates, and virtually annexed the counties of Ulster, Leinster, and Munster, which is to this day, what forms Northern Ireland. The ferocity of his attacks on the Irish landscape branded him, in both folklore and in fact, as the most dreaded man in Irish history.

8. WILLIAM PELHAM KNIGHT OF REIGATE.

I had not intended to digress quite so much into history but the inextricable entwinement of our family with the Irish and the Normans makes it pertinent to our story. It may be a truism that unless you understand where you came from, and where you are, it is impossible to project where you could go.

In the 'Call to Arms' of 1914 William Knight, was rejected for military service due to his physical disability. He had a deformed arm from birth. Four hundred and sixty men from the tiny rural village of Cuckfield did answer the call, and of these, a staggering one in five (81) would never return.

William was the only son of the well-to-do Pelham-Knight family from the Reigate area of Surrey. The Pelham-Knights are an interesting lot. One can arguably trace their ancestry through the Marlborough's' of Duke of Wellington and Churchill fame, back to John Pelham-Knight of Pevensey Castle (1355 -1429). So noted in the *Domesday Book*.

William Knight, as far as we know was the last male in his line, sadly he managed to get himself disowned by the family when on June 26th, 1906 he married Rose Botting of Crawley who was considered to be beneath his station. An impulsive romantic? Perhaps. I like to think so, I would hate to think it was just plain dumb, but who knows.

William and Rose settled at Whiteman's Green – an extension of the town of Cuckfield in Sussex where he worked as a carpenter. Their home was one half of a semi-detached house right across from the Green itself, near the Ship Inn public house. He was a strict God-fearing man, sang in the church choir, and sometimes played the organ in Cuckfield Parish Church.

9. RONALD PELHAM KNIGHT AND SIBLINGS.

When Ronald Pelham Knight - was born December 30, 1916. He was preceded in life and, as it turned out, in death, by three sisters, and a brother, and two more sisters would follow him.

William, Rose, Eddie, Queenie, - Eddy, Ron, Olive, Winn. (Daphne is not born yet)

The eldest sibling was the strikingly beautiful Georgina known as Queenie. She married a farm-worker, Walter Gibbons in 1930. He was from the picturesque village of Porlock in Summerset where they raised three children Rosemary, Heather and David in an amazing thatched roofed stone cottage near the base of the famous

Porlock Hill. Unfortunately, due to the distance between Cuckfield and Porlock the families saw very little of each other in the years that followed.

The second daughter was the free spirited Florence who went by the name of Olive. She married William Southwell in 1929 and I know of no children. In fact we know very little of her as she moved to the north of England, and given the fact that to a man of Sussex, anyone from north of the Thames was a foreigner it is not so surprising. I only met her once, and have the impression of a life-loving party girl. She may have been an actor or a dancer as the few photos I have seen of her show a flamboyant style of dress, lots of fur and feathers.

Next came Winifred, known as Winn. She would wed one of Ron's pals Purse Abbott in 1949. He was a great guy and as Sussex as can be. He mumbled terribly, so much so that it was darn near impossible to understand anything he said. He was arrested once for drunk driving though he rarely touched a drop, because the police just could not make him out. They had one child Valerie and the three of them were all but inseparable. Then one day Val went off to Australia. We were in shock. Not only did she up and leave, but also having got there, she managed to get in tow with some strange Australian person never to return. She had no contact with her Mum and Dad until they finally went out to find her. She and the boyfriend treated them abominably. I believe that both Winn and Purse ultimately died of broken hearts.

Eddy, born Edwin was Ron's only brother in a family of seven children – or eight counting Peggy who lived for just six days. Eddy was a very handsome, thoughtful, gentle sort of person. I believe Ron had to stand up for him from time to time, as he had no inclination towards the rough stuff while Ron quite enjoyed it. Eddy married a wonderful and very proper Welsh girl – Gwen. I swear she stood way under five feet in high-heels. She had the most beautiful, precise, clear, speaking voice. They were blessed with two daughters, Wendy and Elizabeth.

When Ron died in the year 2000 he was survived by two sisters. Edith, we called her Eddie and Daphne – but more of them later.

Ron was actually born at Whiteman's Green, but it is within the parameters of the town of Cuckfield. The dyed in the wool locals will quickly correct you if you call this charming hamlet a village. It once, in 1255, had a Town Charter as a market town, bestowed by Charles II. The village dates back to Norman times. William de Warenne, cousin to the Conqueror, built the Church, which still dominates the landscape to this day, some nine hundred years later.

The building of churches and cathedrals all over England were William the Conqueror's self-imposed penance for the way his troops relentlessly pursued, and slaughtered Harold's army following the battle of Hastings in 1066.

10. CUCKFIELD, SUSSEX.

The Town of Cuckfield was in its own little way a thriving hub of commerce when Ron was growing up. The mode of transportation for many well-off people was still the horse and carriage, while for the average person it was the bicycle if you were lucky enough to own one, or else 'Shanks pony' - you just walked. Since there were no supermarkets around in those days, Cuckfield high street had two butchers, a fishmonger, a grocery store, a green grocer, saddle maker, ironmonger, chemist, newspaper shop, and a barber – in fact every commodity and service that the average person needed was available right there in the village. There were also two doctors' offices, a dentist, policeman, and undertaker, plus a major hospital.

Cuckfield Hospital was actually a relic of a bygone age, known as a Workhouse, where unfortunates were whelped, housed and if not sold into servitude, were worked to death. Charles Dickens in his *Oliver Twist* novel described the lives of those affected and persecuted by the Workhouses.

By the time Ron came along, Cuckfield Hospital had become a modern medical facility serving the whole County of Sussex and beyond.

The main route from London to the popular Edwardian seaside resort of Brighton passed right down Cuckfield High Street. The King's Head Inn at the bottom of the town hill was once the overnight stop for the London to Brighton Stagecoach, that in the 1820s, numbered up to an unimaginable fifty comings and goings a day. But those days were long gone now, and the Town Council's 1825 decision to object to a noisy stinky railroad coming through its town, insisting the proposed site be moved to what is now the much larger town of Hayward's Heath, further halted the growth of the village. Nevertheless, having main arterial roads connecting north, south, east, and west, coming right through Cuckfield kept the town quite busy. Whiteman's Green's only claim to independent historical fame is that the first known Iguanodon fossils (dinosaurs from the Jurassic period) were found right here in 1822.

11. THE SCAR AND SCHOOLDAYS.

It was while Ron as a small child was playing on Whiteman's Green that a wheel came off a passing horse-cart, careened across the road onto the Green smashing into Ron and rolling over his face leaving him with that very distinctive vertical scar and dent on his forehead from eyebrow to hairline. It is a wonder he survived. But I guess God and life had work for him to do. He took a lot of ribbing for the that disfigurement, kids being kids, and it probably contributed to the toughening up that gave him the reputation of someone you did not want to mess with. He actually had a lot of fun with that scar after the war. He got so fed up with strangers asking if he got it in battle that in the end he just said yes and happily drank their offered pint.

Ron Knight was an energetic, gregarious, out-going kid. An adequate student though he favoured the lure of the sports field over the halls of academia. He captained football and cricket teams, and he loved to box. His close pal and sparring partner George Markwick would later enter the professional ring. Ron only got to fight at the local travelling fairgrounds where either up-and-coming or over the hill fighters would take on all comers and the challenger got paid five quid if he lasted three rounds. The odds were usually stacked in favour of the house as the Marquise of Queensbury was noticeably absent, and eye gouging, rabbit punches, and the odd shot to the shorts, were commonplace. Nevertheless, Ron managed to hold his own, and usually came home battered, bruised, with cash.

The village state-run school was, and in fact still is, a magnificent, large sandstone-blocked building situated right next to the Norman church. The headmaster was considered by young Ron to be quite the sadistic character that relished the educational theory of 'spare the rod and spoil the child'. The cane was administered both on the hand and on the rump depending on the offense and the mood. Ron and the more boisterous of his pals the likes of Joe Sears who was also always in trouble, tried every trick in the book to get some relief from the onslaughts. Books inside their shorts and even horsehair laid across the palm of the hand that lore said would split the Cane. I am not sure if any of these worked, mostly they were easily discovered and only resulted in additional punishment.

Ron Snr, William, Eddy.

As with most of his contemporaries from working class families the possibilities of an extended education were slim to none. Poor people were lucky to finish school never mind going to college – that just did not happen for them. The need for each family member to contribute to the cost of every-day living was paramount. Each of the seven Knight children as soon as they were able would go out and do odd jobs to help put food on the table. Vacations did not exist. Adults worked at least six-days a week.

Ron earned money helping at the local farms doing all sorts of things: fruit picking, potato picking, and haymaking, but Pheasant Beating was one of his favourites. The local gentry would have shooting parties when the birds were in season. Small boys would be hired to drive the birds towards the gun-toting toffs. This was done by fanning the boys out in a wide line and moving them across the countryside beating the grass and bushes with long sticks as they went. The pheasant, though it can fly all be it rather cumbersomely, lives on the ground and tends to run very fast from perceived danger until it is clear away from its nest, then it takes to the air with a very noisy flapping of wings to become an easy target for the gentry's twelve-gauge shotguns.

The best part of the hunt was that for a snack, each boy got a 'Plowman's Lunch' comprised of a large bread roll with butter, a massive hunk of Cheddar cheese, some Branston Pickle and a pickled onion – a feast indeed. It was a long day starting before dawn under the disciplined eye of the game-keeper who did not hesitate to swat any child who's natural high spirits impinged on the task at hand. Ron evoked this side of the boss's nature at least once or twice on each hunt.

12. ADOLESCENCE, AND OUT TO WORK.

The family had moved from Whiteman's Green to the new council house subdivision of Glebe Road, I am not exactly sure of the year, it would have been in the mid, Roaring '20s.

Ron had lots of great pals at school, most also lived in Glebe Road, many of whom he would keep all his life. Pretty much all of these friends were also from poor working class families. Their clothes were hand me downs or were made at home by the mothers. Their food was just adequate, never plentiful. There was certainly no room for waste of any kind. His two closest friends were probably John Wrist and George Markwick but stories involving many of the great old families of Cuckfield were also plentiful and enthusiastically passed on around warm fires on cold nights: the Malins, the Replays, the Sayers brothers Joe and Mog, Harry Edwards, Harold Humphries, the Rhodes and Wells brothers, Dick Baird, Charley Pennifold, and many more. I have no idea what happened to John Wrist but I do know that George parlayed his boxing prowess into a teaching career at the very prestigious private school - Ardingly College.

As for the rest of the lads, most of them stayed in the area, and I would grow up with their sons and daughters.

William Knight being a member of the church choir enrolled Ron to join him on Sundays. Ron also earned some pocket money pumping the organ – no double entendre intended! The Church had a magnificent old pipe organ. It was driven not by electricity but by two boys, each on the end of what looked like a child's teeter-totter with handles. Of course, boys being boys they would get tired, bored, start messing around, and the pumping would slow down causing the sound in the church to be akin to a strangled bagpipe. This would draw the ire of the venerable, one-legged Choirmaster Mr. Rapley. He would register his annoyance and get their attention to this fact by thumping on the wood paneling. The boys who lived in some fear of Mr. Rapley would immediately speed up their efforts with the effect that the strains of Rock of Ages agonizingly whined its way back up to some since of normalcy.

The pressure to contribute to the family income drove Ron out of school and he went to work in the village for Green's the fishmonger: filleting, packing, and delivering fish. He was fourteen years old. His first deliveries were made with a horse and cart but he soon went on to use a motorbike and sidecar. Ron loved it. I am told he could roar up the entire length of the High Street with the sidecar wheel off the ground. The word would go out and within minutes, his boss would hear 'That Ronnie Knight is screaming up the High Street again on two wheels'. Ron's father eked out a very poor living doing carpentry. He was never a robust individual health-wise. His wife Rose took to taking in lodgers to help make ends meet. Even though both Queenie and Olive, married and moved out, it is still a mystery to figure out how she accommodated the rest of her family in the house, plus lodgers. But somehow she did.

13. THE DIRTY THIRTIES: RON SIGNS UP.

After William Knight died October 1933 at the youngish age of sixty-one, Bill Hawks (Uncle Bill) became a permanent resident. Bill was a widower, and quite a character. He owned and operated a mobile blacksmith shop and went around the countryside with his tools and equipment in a large horse-drawn caravan. He was a real man of Sussex.

My favourite Bill Hawks story is that one lunch-time he was in the Rose n' Crown having his daily draught, when some chap came running up to him indicating that he should follow him out to the parking lot. There, stone dead was his horse still in the wagon traces. Bill it is reported said 'Well I'll be blowed, that's the first time he's done that.' Bill's only son was Charlie the perennial paperboy. Charlie was a simple soul who delivered his papers late every day, from his old bicycle, served up with his own homespun brand of philosophy. I never met a child, person, or dog that did not love him.

In his latter years, Nellie and Ron would invite Old Bill and a couple of his elderly cronies to our Christmas feast. They would arrive at our front door and sing a brace of old English carols. We all looked forward to it immensely. I can still hum the tunes and know the odd chorus I wish to hell I had written the words down - *'Oh the Mistletoe Bough'* is one that comes to mind.

We were now in the '30s – the 'Dirty 30s' so called to describe the 'Great Depression'. Work of any kind was in short supply. At least Ron had a job at the fishmongers even though it involved long hours and was not very well paid. He and pal John Wrist decided to join the Navy. The pay would be better, it offered a chance to see the world, and it would mean Ron could send a healthy pay packet home to his Mum. John, a year older than Ron, was accepted. Ron's age deception was discovered and he was rejected for being too young. As soon as he was old enough, he tried again to join the armed forces, this time the Army, and on September 3rd 1935, joined the Royal Engineers of the British Regular Army.

Basic Training took place at the Brampton Barracks at Chatham, Kent. The first nine months were typically torturous as are most Basic Training programmes – boot camp. Discipline was strict and unyielding; transgressions drew severe punishment such as the cancellation of leave or cleaning the toilets - with a toothbrush. Yours.

For a lad with Ron's rebellious disposition this was all quite challenging but surprisingly, especially to him, he really enjoyed the life. Along with the hard work, there were lots of sports opportunities and he, being a natural athlete, flourished. The fact that the unit valued the prestige and bragging rights that successful sports endeavours brought, also kept Ron away from a lot of the punishment jobs. He played football, cricket, even table tennis and he boxed.

On completion of Basic Training, he transferred to the 23rd Field Company at Aldershot. When he first arrived, the main form of company transportation was still horse-drawn wagons but soon lorries and motorcycles began to appear. As he was one of the few that had driving experience, and in fact even owned a license he got the job as a trainer. Ron was smart enough to be aware of his own ignorance and lack of education, and was determined to do something about that, so he enrolled in every educational course he could sign up for, making trips to the nearby towns of Gosport and Pangbourne for classes. He developed a real love of reading, and of letter writing - a skill and pleasure that would stay with him for the rest of his life.

In March of 1937 Ron was shipped out to Gibraltar, a peninsular of land ceded to Great Britain by Spain in 1713 and declared a British colony in 1830. The brutal Spanish Civil War was in full swing between the Republicans and Franco's Nationalists. The Strait of Gibraltar is the only western entrance to the Mediterranean Sea, which in turn leads to the Far East via the Suez Canal. As such, the strategic importance of this little British colony made it paramount for the British Government to maintain a strong military presence on The Rock.

Though England was officially neutral in the Spanish conflict, many 'advisors' and volunteers were loaned to the Republicans in their struggle against Franco's revolutionaries - all to no avail as General Franco prevailed, retired the Monarchy, and formed a dictatorial fascist government that would last for forty-one years.

14. Nellie Engebretsen.

September 1938 found Ron home for some leave. His pal Mog Sayers' girl friend Rene talked him into meeting a friend of hers, a beautiful young Irish girl be the name of Ellen Christina Engebretsen. 'Nellie'.

She and Ron became an immediate item. She was born the eldest of seven surviving children to an Irish mother Ellen Sullivan and a Norwegian father Martin Engebretsen. Nellie, being a teenager in the Dirty Thirties, and like so many of her countrymen and women, left her home to seek a better life for herself, and a source of steady income to send home to her family. She sailed far away across the Irish Sea, or so it must have seemed in those days, to England. You have to understand that in those times there was no safety net for her to fall back on. She could not phone home to her Mum and Dad and get them to send her a couple of quid. There were neither phones nor spare pounds available. She was on her own in what must have seemed to a young Catholic girl a strange, hostile, and heathen land.

These mostly undereducated young girls usually wound up either working on the land, in hospitals or 'in-service', a term that described servants in a large estate's household. Nellie was employed in the latter; she worked as a housemaid for a family living in a beautiful country mansion on the back road between Cuckfield and Hayward's Heath. I believe that Nellie was a very bright, intelligent individual and I suspect that in another time, space, and place she might have had an interesting and sparkling career. She was very attractive, and curious about anything and everything. But for those such as her a career was never an option. She was a very strong woman with a tremendous sense of purpose. When she put her mind to something – watch out. Nellie always liked to look nice. She had a straight back, good figure, brown eyes, and thick, dark auburn hair framing a face blessed with flawless skin. She needed and used very little makeup. I do not think her pride in appearance was so much vanity as it was a great sense of inner dignity and self-respect.

15. WHILE WAR CLOUDS GATHER.

In October of '38 Ron got word that his younger sister Eddie had married one of his Mum's lodgers John Ryder. John was a dashing good-looking young Errol Flynn type. He played trumpet and had his own band. He and Eddie became wonderful ballroom dancers and later in life would become instructors. Eddie would always be dressed up to the nines. Bleached blonde hair, lots of make-up short skirts with lots of petticoats - she was wonderful. They would be childhood sweethearts until the day he died. They just could not leave each other alone. 'Misterkins' and 'Misseskins' they called each other – sounds yuk doesn't it? But you had to know them. They had three children, John, Barry and Daphne.

In early 1939 the war clouds were gathering in Europe and it was beginning to look like England would inevitably be drawn into a conflict. Hitler was demanding the return of all lands that were given up by Germany in their much-hated Treaty of Versailles that ended the First World War. This stupid piece of political overkill had disaster written all over it. It was significant to England's potential entanglement with the politics of Europe that these disputed territories were now part of both France and Poland. England of course had defence treaties with both of these countries.

Britain declared war on Germany September 1st, 1939 the day after Hitler invaded Poland. The modern German war machine employed tactics hitherto unheard of, combining land and air forces in a disciplined coordinated attack called the Blitzkrieg. They were unstoppable and quickly overran Western Europe.

16. LIFE ON THE ROCK. HUNT THE BISMARCK.

Ron's two years in Gibraltar prior to the outbreak of war, were mostly spent doing work that modernized its defenses. Geographic positioning and the physical Rock itself made it a natural fortress. The Colony is joined to Spain to the north by a flat causeway that is just above sea level and upon which is situated the airport. To the south is the Straits of Gibraltar a mere 14.5 km of water separating Europe and Algeciras in North Africa. Whoever controls the Rock controls all sea-going movements of goods from East to West, including the lifeblood of any modern civilization – oil.

The Royal Engineers were given the task of building and replacing heavy artillery batteries high up on the Rock, facing the Straits. There were no decent roads to get up there, only a trail that even self-respecting goats gave a pass to. Ron 'volunteered' to drive a truck up, take an old gun down, and then drive back up pulling a modern artillery piece. There were places where they had to rig a sling from the rock face above to hold the outside edge of the truck while the inside wheels moved the vehicle forward inch by inch. The job got done.

Once again, it was Ron's sporting prowess that got him preferential treatment, and landed him the nice cushy job of driver to the Chief Engineer, Colonel Fordham. This led to chauffeuring three successive Governors: Lord Gort, Field Marshal Ironsides, and General Liddle. His popularity in this position kept him on The Rock serving additional tours of duty for a couple of years.

When Anthony Eden the British Foreign Secretary (one day to become Sir Anthony Eden, Prime Minister of England) did an inspection of Gibraltar in 1941 Ron got the call to drive for him. They apparently got along very well, so much so that Mr. Eden on hearing that Ron had not had leave for two years arranged for him to hitch a ride on the light cruiser HMS London that was due to leave on May 19, 1941 to escort an evacuee ship the SS Arundel Castle, to Clyde in Scotland. Little did he know, that the previous day, the Pocket Battleship Bismarck escorted by the heavy cruiser Prinz Eugin had been spotted 'breaking out' into the North Sea. At this time, Britain was losing the battle for the Atlantic. The German U-Boats 'Wolf Packs' were savaging the vital supply lines from America.

The very thought of having the most powerful battleship in the world on the loose was too bitter to contemplate. The Bismarck was an amazing machine. It could match the speed of any British light cruiser while outgunning their largest battleships. A formidable combination

The English Home Fleet was scrambled to find, intercept, and destroy this German threat. On the morning of May 24, the pride of the British Navy, the Battle Cruiser HMS Hood engaged the Bismarck in the Denmark Straits, between Iceland and Greenland. The Hood received two salvos, one from Prinz Eugin which did little damage, the second from Bismarck. She broke in two and sank within minutes, leaving three survivors from a crew of 1,419, and England in shocked disbelief.

The British had survived the Blitz, they had fought and won the Battle of Britain, thwarting Germany's attempt at destroying their air force and air defenses. In the process, they bought precious time to rebuild and supply an army that had all but been destroyed at Dunkirk. Bear in mind that the attack on Pearl Harbor was still six months away. The US was not yet in this fight, other than making American fortunes from the sale of supplies. The rest of Europe lay conquered. The tiny islands of Britain supported by its commonwealth allies stood alone.

The word came down from Sir Winston Churchill "I don't care how you do it, you must sink the Bismarck". The impetus was as much to restore national pride and moral, as it was to neutralize this very real military threat, and I guess I should throw a whiff of vengeance in there too.

The Bismarck hounded by as many war ships as England could muster, detached Prinz Eugin to confuse and split the pursuit forces. It headed west. The Bismarck turned south.

Gibraltar was home base to the British Mediterranean Fleet a battle group led by the aircraft carrier Ark Royal. She was dispatched to search for Bismarck and joining that search was HMS Dorsetshire, a heavy cruiser escorted by the cruiser HMS London - with Ron on board. It was Swordfish airplanes from Ark Royal, refueled on the carrier HMS Victorious that damaged the steering system of Bismarck, which would be the beginning of its end. The amazing pilots of these slow-moving, diminutive, twin winged plywood and canvas planes, flew at sea level straight at the guns of their target to let loose their torpedoes.

After heavy, relentless bombardment of the great but crippled ship by the British Navy, the Dorsetshire, on May 27th, finished off Bismarck with torpedoes and picked up 111 of the 116 survivors out of a crew of 2,200. Hood was avenged.

Following the battle, the HMS London immediately received orders to break off and sail south to perform other escort duties. Ron was eventually dropped off way down on the East coast of Africa at Bathurst in Gambia to wait for a passage home that he eventually got, arriving in England on July 12, 1941.

So finally he got his leave, and time being of the essence, Ron and Nellie were married on July 19, 1941 at St. Paul's Church in Hayward's Heath. It was such short notice that they had to scramble to complete a wedding party.

17. Bomb Disposal: Ron's Lads.

His next job was that of dispatch rider for the 275th Field Company RE, attached to the 51st Highlanders of El Alamein fame. He then went on to the 263 Field Company at Maidstone where he was employed to train new conscripts. I think he really liked this work but unfortunately as things would happen, he had a 'falling out' with his Company Commander – now there's a big bloody surprise! He was given the choice of transferring to either an Assault Engineer unit or to a Bomb Disposal unit. He chose the latter because he would be stationed closer to Cuckfield, and joined the 23rd BD – 96 Section and after six weeks training in Westward Ho, Devon, he arrived at Ashford in Kent.

Now a by-product of the bombing 'Blitz' of England was thousands of unexploded bombs all over eastern and southeast England. Bomb Disposal's job was to locate them and either neutralize or detonate them. Airfields were a high priority as they had been prime targets for bombing and of course were direly needed by the RAF. Ron's work was mostly in around London and throughout the South East. It was nerve-racking, dangerous work at which it was considered a good day's work to return to the unit with the same number of men that went out. Under this constant pressure, the men quickly formed into a tight unit. They trained hard in order to reduce their risk factors down to a minimum. During this intense period Ron got on well with all ranks and kept fond memories of some of the lads that were special to him: Evens their driver from Tiger Bay in Wales, Smith, Hargraves, Les (Bonny) Gunner and Fitzgerald. There was also Ward, who could not read or write, how he got in the army is another story. There was the hulking Ted Delahunty, a great pal who came from a large family of all boys in Liverpool, and there was a wee young Scot by the name of Box.

18. Amid Threat of Invasion: Sheila.

As 1941 slid into '42, the constant threat of a German invasion meant that along with disposing of bombs, it was also part of their job to prepare for the worst and make sure that the enemy would not have anywhere to land planes in support of the inevitable amphibian invasion should one take place. So, his group was given the task of preparing two of our airfields in Kent for demolition under such circumstance. This included wiring up runways, administration buildings, living quarters, and hangers. It was difficult and important work and Ron remembers feeling quite honoured that he was given the job to head up this initiative ahead of many more-senior NCOs. Within two weeks, he was able to report that both fields could be demolished either electronically or via hand-lit fuses all at very short notice.

With all the talk of invasion, and the continued, albeit sporadic bombing, Ron had sent Nellie home to Ireland to have her baby.

It was while working on one of the airfields that he got word that Nellie had given him a 3lb 4oz daughter on April 1st, 1942. Surprise! April fool! 'Sheila' had not been due till the beginning of June. It would be remembered as one of the happiest days of his life.

Nellie came from the very picturesque town of Cobh in County Cork, Eire. Cobh (pronounced Cove), known as the Great Island, is indeed a large island in the middle of Cork harbour, the second largest natural harbour in the world next to Sydney, Australia. It has several claims to fame, as it was the last place where passengers could board the great liners of this age, who plied between Europe and the Americas. It was the last port of call for both the ill-fated Lusitanian and the great Titanic.

19. BOMBS AWAY, BOMBS AT HOME.

The next task for bomb disposal was clearing minefields along the Kent coast that had mostly been laid down by the Canadians in such a lackadaisical manor that the maps they provided were useless. His group suffered more casualties doing this work than they ever had disposing of enemy bombs. The life expectancy for an active Sapper in bomb disposal at this time was seven weeks! While working at this, he was called away to deal with a particularly difficult problem - a suspected bombsite in extremely soft and boggy ground. He actually ended up digging down fifty-six feet to reach a 500lb bomb and defuse it. At the time, it was the deepest excavation of a live bomb ever recorded.

From Ashford they were sent to a base in Winchester to bolster the ranks of Bomb Disposal units that were suffering heavy casualties in the Portsmouth and Southampton dock areas.

While at Winchester he was called up to a town called Barton Stacy where several civilians had been killed or injured by some very odd looking and hitherto unidentified explosive objects. This was his first introduction to the devastating Butterfly Bombs also known as Cluster Bombs. These anti-personnel weapons were dropped in clusters of twenty-three and each one had half a pound of TNT explosive in it. About the size of a small soup can, they were a particularly unpredictable and sensitive piece of unexploded ordinance. After considering several options including the use of a 303 Enfield rifle he decided to try lassoing one of these little buggers with a long piece of rope and then giving the rope a jerk. This actually worked fine except that the other bombs in the immediate area tended to blow up with it in sympathy.

One time when working on a cluster bomb site, he noticed one of the bombs did not detonate, it just sat there on the side of a pathway leading to a retirement home. He waited, threw a few rocks at it and then according to witnesses he just went over and gave the bloody thing a swift kick. No kidding. Fortunately, nothing happened, and later, when taking this bomb apart he found that it was missing its detonator. After much investigation and deliberation he concluded that there was absolutely no way to safely dismantle these bombs and gave notice to his higher-ups that no attempt should be made to disarm them and that they must always be detonated.

He kept no record of how many bombs and mines his team worked on during this period, but they must have numbered in the many hundreds. Every time they were confronted with a new type of bomb, it was trial and error time in its most terrifying form. Each procedure was called out by the performer and documented by another member of the team. Many boys died leaving details so others might live.

20. Prepare for the Assault on Europe.

Then came October 1943. The boys were moved down to Westward Ho for intensive training in preparation for the much-anticipated amphibious invasion of continental Europe. There were thousands of troops assembled, forming a Combined Operation Group consisting of contingents from all the allied countries. Ron's group, the 96 Section was made up of one officer Lt. J.E.A. Deacon, one Sergeant, two Corporals, one driver/cook, and twenty-six Sappers. They were the only Bomb Disposal unit to be used on the initial assault on what would be called Gold Beach.

Of course at this time they had no idea of where they were going never mind where they would land. The code names for the beaches were all top secret, learned at the last minute, and even then only on a need to know basis. Their job was described as crossing the beach scaling a steep embankment, clearing mines and booby traps as they went to provide a wide swath in which other sections of the Royal Engineers and Signals could bring ashore a cross channel cable in order to establish direct communications with central command in England.

The work had to be carried out in awful conditions. The late winter of 1943 was downright nasty. It was bloody cold and it rained just about every day. As it turned out this was perfect training for what was to come. They did however have good food, and most nights a dry sleep, billeted in a Butlin's Holiday Camp.

The intensity of their training was no kids' stuff. They practiced what they had to do repeatedly. Sometimes staying out for over twenty-four hours at a time. Both the landing and the job to be done when they got there were worked on, all on a similar beach to the one they expected to arrive at on the other side. Ron's group took this work very seriously and indeed took great pride in it. They were supremely confidant that their mission would be accomplished and that they would make a difference. His sub-section with the addition of one more corporal was picked to go in with the first assault group. The three other sub-sections were assigned to other groups.

21. Last leave.

Ron grabbed eight days leave in February and spent them with his lovely wife and baby in Ireland.

By the spring the rumours of the Allied invasion were running rampant, it seemed that every person they met had a new handle on what was what. That being what may, it was clear to every soldier that this massive build up had to go somewhere pretty soon or run the risk of imploding on itself. One thing was for sure; Ron knew when he took this leave that he was not going to see his family again for some time.

Nellie's brother Matty had met him at the station in Cobh he recognized Ron from photos and greeted him enthusiastically. Unfortunately due to Matt's strong Irish accent, Ron could not understand one word he said. Actually, that is not quite true, the word 'pint' came up and they both embraced not only the sentiment but also several of the facts.

For the rest of this eight-day trip Ron says he did not want to let Nellie and Sheila out of his sight. It was a magic time for them. Amazingly, time spent together since they met in 1938 had been merely a series of six to ten-day leaves. Though this was no different for him then for a complete generation of young Brits, it was indeed an odd way to begin married life. The only real plans that could be made were what they might do on the next leave. Their relationship was built through love letters. Ron was a great letter-writer and I believe from having read some of his writings, an incurable romantic. I guess the combination was an endearing factor in what must have amounted to a long, three-year, intermittently interrupted honeymoon.

22. Ready, steady, and go.

Back to work, the Section was moved to a village near Brentwood in Essex and it was from there, at the Chatham docks that Ron took a course in deep-sea diving, underwater bomb-disposal, and demolition. It was the crashiest of crash courses making him 'qualified' in three weeks. Once again, he embraced the work and made every effort to be as competent in as many aspects of the job as he could possibly be in the available time. He could disarm most pieces of common ordinance with his eyes closed. This attitude and attention to detail really paid off for him on the other side and he attributes it to saving his life on more than one occasion when he found himself working in pitch black conditions both under-ground and under water.

At the peak of preparedness, in this the last camp before what was now being called D-Day the orders were to get as much rest as possible. Regardless of that directive, Ron had his men doing five mile runs alternating with ten mile marches on successive days, all in full battle order (that's 55 lbs). They were determined to be just as fit as the amazing and very macho Navy Commandos with whom they had been training.

On May 1st they were marched to yet another 'last camp' which they had been told was some ways away but in fact turned out to be just two miles outside Brentwood. It was all part of the secrecy thing. The camp was all under canvas and it housed over one hundred thousand men. They were locked-in under heavy guard at all entrances and subject to constant patrols. The fear of leaks of information about troops and troop movement was beyond paranoia. They were indeed taking no chances. The men just had to make their own amusements in the camp. They had sports events, they gambled, had sing-a-longs, anything to break the monotony of routine and to keep tensions as low as possible. It was a long month in which no contact of any kind was allowed with the outside world.

Then, one morning, it suddenly came over the loudspeaker system - the word they had all been waiting for, that 96 Section Bomb Disposal was to report immediately to the command post in full battle kit. Every few minutes another unit was called and put onto buses to go to the Lord knew where. It turned out to be Tilbury docks where at 5pm they started loading onto a Belgian ship, the SS

Leopoldville. A U-boat would sink this brave, hard working little ship on Christmas Eve of that year, just off Charbourg.

At 8pm accompanied by seven other troop ships and six navy escorts the mini armada left the dock. It was June 2. The ship was so crowded you could hardly turn around. He felt a mixture of fear for what was now imminent, and a kind of relief that it was finally underway. The on-again off-again rumours were getting to everyone and tempers were stretched pretty thin. Their course took them east down the River Thames estuary and then south through the Strait of Dover where they were welcomed to Europe by being shelled by the German defenses on the French coast a few miles away. Keeping in mind that Germany had made massive preparations for this invasion that they believed would come via the shortest route – the Pas de Calais. Any movement of shipping in the Straits would trigger an immediate response from the coastal defenses and indeed, it did.

The flotilla now turned west along the English Channel and hove-to at a point just behind the Needles at the western tip of the Isle of Wight. It was pitch black, rough seas and raining like hell. It seemed more like October than June.

After yet another restless night on board he awoke, went up on deck to find the surrounding area nothing but wall-to-wall ships of every nationality and description. He could not believe his eyes; he had never seen anything like it. Tenders from the mainland were scurrying around with supplies and loading them onto the anchored ships. Some ships, including his, were taking landing craft aboard. The men were mustered and each received fifty francs in 'liberation money' though they still had no idea where they were actually going. Some said they were headed north and would attack right at the German coast, some said that the French Riviera or even Italy was the destination. Some thought the French money they had just been given could be all part of the secrecy bluff, designed to confuse spies. No letters had been allowed in or out of the camps for over many weeks.

23. June 6, 1944: D-Day (The Longest Day)

In the early hours of June 6, though at the time he admits to having no idea what day it was anymore, the ship he was on quietly weighed anchor and moved out into the stormy channel. The weather was atrocious. They had a prayer service on deck at which everyone was very quiet, each absorbed with his own private thoughts, and each not wanting by word or look, betray his innermost fears. Ron and his pals Delohunty and Gunner had made a pact to keep an eye on Box, the nineteen-year old. They all kept close together. As they got out into open water, it became clear that they were heading down the French coast and certainly not north to Calais as most had anticipated.

It was the most surreal feeling he had ever encountered. As they crashed up and down in the heavy swells, in every direction as far as the eye could see were hundreds of ships of all descriptions. Above their heads wave upon wave of warplanes —bombers with their fighter cover, filled the skies. The noise was indescribable. It actually helped in a way as it gave them confidence in that they were part of something really strong and powerful.

They were loaded into a landing craft that was lashed to the ship's side. There were about 140 men in his boat. Along with his Bomb Disposal Unit was the Commando 47 of the Royal Marines who would have the unenviable task of covering his men while they did their job. As they all hunched in the boat double-checking their equipment he heard a few of the commandos chatting away. Incredulously at a time like this they were arguing as to who was the best singer Sinatra or Crosby. Ron never forgot it, he recalled thinking to himself how lucky he was to have such tough, fearless men as these looking out for his crew. The seas seemed to be getting worse instead of better and the landing craft was awash with seawater and vomit.

About a mile or so from the beach, their landing craft was launched from the lee side of the ship. And now were on their own with no turning back, and to God knew what ahead. There were certainly few options and in truth right now, they would have done anything to get themselves out of this pitching craft and just get on with it.

24. The Landing – Gold Beach.

The plan had been to land on the beach at low tide in front of the defence obstacles that littered the beaches. But they were late. You would have to wonder how with all this high-powered planning they could be strategically late. Germany had four years to prepare 'Fortress Europe' for this invasion and part of that preparation were these formations of welded steel I-beams that sat in the sand and protruded ten feet high at low tide.

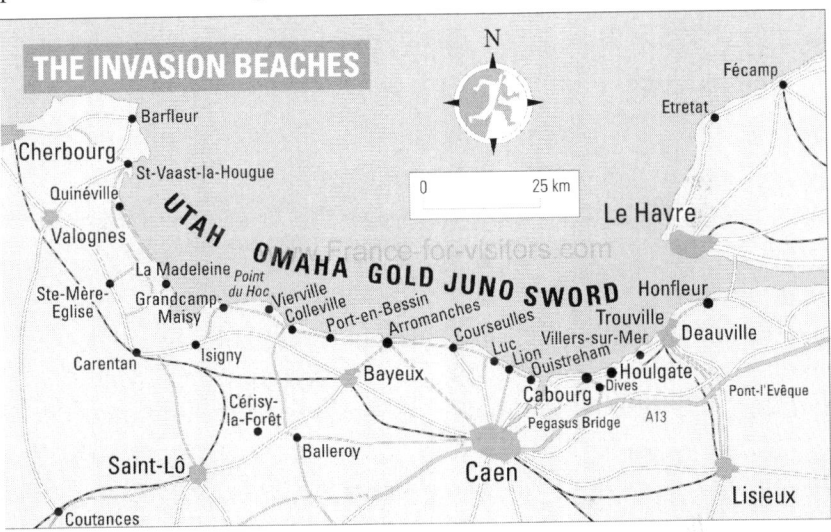

As they got closer to the beach, it became clear that they were not going to hit land in front of them as had been anticipated; instead, they were going to land right on top of them. They were late and the tide was running in fast. The beach was already beginning to look like a scrap heap. There was debris everywhere. Bodies of fallen comrades floated among the half submerged equipment, including trucks and tanks. Yes, floating tanks nicknamed Ducks, in the rough seas did not in fact float; many did not make it to shore.

There was a sudden shuddering bang and the next thing he knew he was up to his chin in seawater, they had hit the gun turret of a submerged tank and their landing craft was almost ripped in half throwing men, equipment and bodies into the sea. Perhaps he was lucky in that the lowering of the front ramp on a landing craft gave the defenders a focal point for their machine guns – many young men never touched the beach alive. Mortar shells were exploding all over the place; there was the rattle of machine gun bullets plus the deadly 88mm canons. Overhead there was strafing from the Luftwaffe in between their being engaged by Allied fighters. There was the pounding of our air forces on the German defenses. Every gun on every ship was firing at will, amounting to thousands of salvos thundering through the smoke-filled skies.

As he waded through the surf he noticed that Dalhaunty had hold of young Box by the back of his jacket so Ron went over and got hold of the other side. Every couple of feet they lifted the diminutive Scot's head clear of the water so he could gulp a few breaths of air before submerging again. Believe it or not, Ron recalls finding some humour in this.

To have any real understanding of these events you should study a map and do some independent reading on the subject. The movies *The Longest Day* for its chronology of the landings, and *Saving Private Ryan* for its realism are well worth a visit.

The invasion of Europe was an immense undertaking in which there was no guarantee of the outcome. The whole continent of Europe was a veritable fortress and the German High Command had had four years to prepare for the attack they knew must come eventually. They called their coastal defenses the Atlantic Wall. It is well known in military circles that it requires a minimum of twice as many men to successfully attack a position as it does to defend one, so the first peril for the Allies was to escape being annihilated on the beaches before they could land sufficient men and equipment to take on an experienced and entrenched enemy.

The most likely place for the Allies to invade was straight across the Channel at its narrowest point the Pas-de-Calais. The distance was short, only twenty-one miles, so the element of surprise due to the quick assault time seemed to benefit the attackers. The architects of the Allied invasion (Operation Overlord) took advantage of this predictability. Their strategy was to proliferate the belief in that concept by all and any means that would reinforce the notion that that is where the invasion would take place. All the while the real plan called for the invasion to be much further south, on the beaches of Normandy an area called the bay of the Seine that stretches west from Le Havre to Cherbourg, a span of about 100km in total width.

They divided the landing beaches into five landing areas, each assigned to various Allied divisions with very specific targets and missions. In the East was Sword mostly British with French contingents, to their West was Juno comprised of the Canadians, then Gold mostly British, and then the two American beaches of Omaha and Utah.

25. Get the hell off the beaches.

Phase One. The first objective of course was not to be slaughtered on the beaches and to establish landing zones or 'beachheads'. Next, strike inland with all speed and connect with other allied divisions, relieving the airborne troops that had been dropped by parachute and gliders behind enemy lines to capture and hold key bridges and road intersections.

Ron's unit waded out of the crashing surf and scrambled up the beach onto dry land. There were explosions all around them with the ping of bullets and shrapnel ricocheting of rocks and equipment. Their training kicked in. They just put their minds to doing their jobs and left everything else to take care of itself. They were so scared that in truth there was an unreal or surreal numbness that seemed to transcend that fear. Slowly the division was able to move off the beach clearing mines as they went under fire the whole time, and move inland. They spent their first night in the small town of Tracy-sur-Mer. Next day their Marine guardians left them to proceed west and attack the German positions at Port-en-Bessin from the rear.

Gold beach was situated between the towns of Port-en-Bessin and La Riviere and had the US landing at Omaha 24km to the west, and the Canadians at Juno to the east. The forces in the initial assault on Gold, along with Commando 47, were the 50th infantry division (Northumberland) - all were part of the 30th British Army Corps (XXX Corp) and it in turn was part of the British 2nd Army.

Phase Two. The 'breakout' from Normandy - swing east then north to capture all the French and Dutch bridges that crossed the major rivers and canals that would allow the enemy to retreat back into Germany, where they might in defence of their homeland, organize a substantial counter-attack. Easy to say and it may sound all very simple, but it was not. There were horrendous battles, attacks, defeats, and counter-attacks pitting two enormous forces against one another both sides furious, experienced and determined. There were also terrible mistakes made on both sides that resulted in unthinkable destruction of property and life, both military and civilian.

The rest of XXX Corp moved southwest to join the attack on Caen from the east. Montgomery and The British force's failure to take the hub city of Caen on D-Day would prove to be a significant setback for the Allies. It allowed the German units in and around the city, and in particular the very experienced and powerful 21st Panzer Division to reinforce, solidify and plan counter offensives. The defence of the city that was a crossroads hub, brought further Allied advances around and up into France and Holland to a standstill.

Ron's group was diverted to a brutal battle that was taking place at the town of Tilly-sur-Seulles 20km west of Caen. General Horrocks commander of the XXX Corp launched the attack the morning of June 10th. The area was strongly defended by the Panzer-Lehr-Division. The Allies entered the town on June 11th but were thrown right back. It would take another five-days, nearly a thousand Allied lives and saturation bombing by the US Air force to capture what was left of the town with a loss of just two-hundred and thirty two German troops.

26. BONNY.

During this battle on June 10th, Ron's team was clearing a minefield that went up a steep 100ft rise. The way they were set up was that Sapper (Bonny) Gunner was in the lead with the mine detector that looks like a frying pan with a long walking stick of a handle. This device, through electronic sensors made a crackling noise in his earphones if it detected metal. His job was to find the mine. Ron followed and would uncover and defuse the ordinance. The rest of the team would dig the mine out, take it away and mark the cleared path with bright tape for others to safely follow through the minefield.

On this fateful day about three quarters of the way up the rise Bonny must have stumbled or who knows exactly what. He may have hit the mine or a trip-wire with the detector and realizing what he had done, threw himself on top of the mine. Almost before Ron could fully comprehend what had taken place there was an explosion and his friend all but disintegrated before his eyes. Parts of Bonny landed on him but somehow the shrapnel missed him, other than ripping the arm badges off his sleeve. The blast hit the officer behind Ron, in the face and chest, while knocking another Sapper back down the hill.

They got medical help for the wounded and buried Sapper Gunner in a temporary grave. He would letter be laid to rest in the military cemetery in Bayeux. This historic town was the home of William the Conqueror, and the famous Bayeux Tapestry that depicts the Battle of Hastings from the Norman perspective.

The loss of Bonny was without a doubt the most profound event in Ron's war for so many reasons. He was a very close friend; they called him 'Bonny the smiling boy' because though he loved to laugh, he always took his job so seriously. There was no doubt in Ron's mind that he would not have survived if Bonny had not sacrificed himself. Throughout the rest of his life Ron would be Bonny's *Private Ryan*, someone to whom he owed living a good life, a life that would always put more in then it would take out.

Ron wrote a fine letter, something he always excelled at, to Bonny's family and got a marvelous one back from his sister Kitty. Ron described how his hero died but obviously without any gory details. He assured them that their boy had died instantly and in the most heroic manner known to mankind, that of laying down his life for his mates. Ron would visit the gravesite near the end of his life and was totally overwhelmed by the experience.

27. THE GERMANS HOLD AND BATTLE FOR CAEN.

When one thinks of a retreat one imagines one group running while being hotly pursued by another group. The military events following the Normandy landings were not even close to this concept. The German retreat was a brilliant military tactical maneuver that was designed to achieve an organized withdrawal while inflicting maximum punishment on the pursuers. They would faint back and trap the allies in pockets. They would thrust forward stalling the advance, and then just disappear under cover of darkness.

Looking at the war in Europe from a distance it might seem that it was all simply a case of effecting the D-Day landings of the Allied forces and driving the German army out. Not quite. Not even close. The outcome would not be assured for another six months of constant battle. The Allies faced an enormous army which in the beginning was larger than their own, and was both experienced and determined.

For the next week it seemed that Ron's unit moved forward two miles and then were pushed back one mile. Progress was very slow and provisions of all kinds were in short supply. This shortage changed dramatically on the 14th of June when a Mulberry Harbour, an amazing devise that was in fact a floating harbour was towed across the channel and installed at Arromanches. This allowed for a massive landing and build up of men and equipment to feed the stretched Allied supply lines.

There were no easy landings on the beaches of Normandy but the Americans, particularly on Omaha beach, had the worst of it. The beach was short and met with high cliffs that had to be scaled under unbelievably heavy enemy fire that was directed straight down at them. This area also happened to be particularly well armed and defended. The result was that the whole Allied attack was being held up on its Western flank that in turn put heavy pressure on the British sectors that had the additional job of making sure the Germans could not reinforce their troops that were facing the Americans.

Eventually the US, with terrible losses, did prevail and began to move out south and east. The German army gave nothing up easily and the battle for Caen went on and on with massive loss of lives on both sides. It would take another six weeks of bitter fighting to finally take the city.

During the Battle of Caen, on July 17th, a British Spitfire northeast of the city strafed the commander of the German defenses of Western Europe, Field Marshal Erwin Rommel's staff car. Rommel was badly injured. He survived only to be implicated in the unsuccessful July 20th assassination attempt on Hitler. He was offered a honourable suicide in return for good treatment for his family. He died from cyanide Oct. 14th.

Ron's unit moved into the city, their work in Caen included sweeping for booby-traps that the retreating army had left for them. The enemy was quite inventive and very deadly. Ron found explosive devices in biscuit tins, toilet tanks, and even teddy bears. Though the results from the explosion of these devices were deadly enough they were for the most part only on a small scale, the main purpose of these weapons was to undermine moral, slow the offensive down and waste resources. In this they were very effective.

One afternoon while working on a house that had been the HQ for the German Artillery, there in the basement, he found and defused a bomb that was set for a full seven days hence. It was large enough to demolish half the street if it had gone off. Interestingly, while de-booby-trapping this house he came across a detailed map of Sussex with Cuckfield specifically marked on it. For what purpose we will never know, maybe just for the need to control the major arterial east-west corridor of the A272 Road. He gave the map to his officer and never did discover its significance.

I once asked Dad what was the most frightening part of those days. He said that if you had time to think about it everything was scary. The Mortars were deadly accurate and devastating, there were snipers everywhere, and the sound of the 88mm is something he still hears in his sleep. But the most feared was the sound of the RAF Typhoon dive-bombers who he swears struck at anything that moved. They came out of the sky from thousands of feet up and screamed straight down at you letting loose their rockets before pulling out to strafe with their Browning machine guns. Fighting through the hedgerow countryside was also particularly scary as with the ebb and flow of so many mini and even large battles it was hard to know exactly where the enemy lines were at any given time. The noise you heard behind a hedge could be friend or foe!

28. THE BREAKOUT: CLOSING THE FALAISE GAP

After Caen, the XXX Corp moved east, capturing Caumont-l'evente on July 29th and advanced on the hub town of Vire August 6th. At the same time, the Germans launched a major counter-attack attempting to strike west through Mortain to the coastal town of Avranches, driving a wedge between the American and British forces. This attack turned out to be a disaster for the German 7th Army. It was undermanned for such a maneuver and the offensive was held and pushed back by the American forces, backed by considerable air superiority.

Hitler insisted that his troops continue to attack and fight for every inch of real estate, even though the wisdom of his own commanders would have been to withdraw across the rivers into Germany and there make a stand. If they had just done this, the outcome of the war could have been different. Germany may have held long enough to negotiate a more reasonable surrender in exchange for the saving of countless lives. It was not to be.

As the Germans fell back, they were engaged by three forces: the Americans moving east and north, the British coming south, and the Canadians coming southwest. The Germans were all but surrounded in an area near the city of Falaise, it became known as the Falaise Pocket. The war could have ended right there. The Allies failure to close the gap allowed a large part of the retreating German 7th Army to move east through the only escape route, which was heroically held open for them to fight another day.

Montgomery would be severely criticized by historians for his failure to close the trap. The Falaise action lasted from August 12th to 21st and its partial success signaled the end of the Battle for Normandy. The Allies had finally landed over 600,000 men who at any time could have had to face von Rundstedt's potential army of over 800,000. If the German High Commander had been allowed by Hitler to commit his total force to Rommel instead of holding back reserves for the landing at the Pas-de-Calais that never came, who knows what the outcome might have been. As it was, the cost: killed, wounded, captured or missing - The Allies 226,386 and for Germany as many as 400,000 of which over half were POWs.

29. Liberation: Holland & Belgium.

Ron's outfit followed the German retreat north. They had the job of clearing mines from the roads left behind be the withdrawing army. He crossed the Seine on August 25th near Vernon via one of the floating bridges built by the Royal Engineers. Within five days, the last of the German Army had itself retreated across the Seine at various points along the line.

Ron was then sent on loan to the Guards Armoured Division who crossed the Somme Valley and pushed through the Belgium boarder at Tournai heading to the liberation of Brussels on September 3rd.

After Brussels, Ron's unit dropped back to a town called Oudenaarde where he waited for four days for his Section to catch up with him. It was actually a wonderful break. It was the first time that he had a chance to reflect on the fact that he was doing something important and meaningful. The Belgium people were so warm and kind to them. He was invited to two big civic receptions. At one of them, members of the resistance were honoured; including a seventeen-year old girl who was credited with having rescued dozens of our pilots and paratroopers, and getting them back to our lines.

Next job was back to Brussels where he was assigned to clear the Queen's Palace of unexploded bombs. He found twelve of them in total and defused them all. One of them was some twenty feet down and while working on it, the excavation caved in on him. His mates dug him free and pulled him to safety with just a broken nose to show for it, and he was back at work the following day. Interestingly, for this work, the Belgium government awarded his officer a medal. Ron would also be honoured with a medal for this work but some sixty-years later.

September 4th saw the liberation of Antwerp. That meant the Allies now held most of inland France and formed a semicircle from Caen to Antwerp entrapping large numbers of German forces and equipment in the remaining, occupied coastal ports.

Liberating the city of Antwerp was one thing. Securing the port and estuary were something else. This task went to the Canadians, and like so many of their tasks, it seems they drew a very short straw. There was no cover whatsoever. A flat, open, boggy area of land surrounded the extremely well defended port. They took horrendous casualties but as expected, and as usual, got the job done. They fought with great honour and distinction.

The Allies now pushed from the south, southwest, and northeast, back towards the channel ports. Ron's unit liberated Gent and then moved back into France to attack the small town of Lille September 5th, one of the last German pockets of strong resistance in France.

There was still lots of tough fighting to be done, as the seaports all fell one be one to the Allies: Le Havre September 12th, Boulogne September 22nd, and Calais six-days later.

Meanwhile Ron's section was fully occupied with bridges. They were either building them or clearing them of explosive devices. Some bridges had been rigged for demolition and then either abandoned or booby-trapped. It was intense work.

30. Market-Garden – A Bridge Too Far.

It was always very apparent that bridges were the key to further success in ending the war. There were still significant German forces in parts of Holland, southern Belgium, and Luxemburg. If these armies could be held or delayed from returning to Germany intact, they could be dealt with by the growing Allied armies who were backed by mounting, superior air power.

An ambitious plan was developed with the code name Market-Garden. The plan had two parts.

Part one was Market. It called for daring airborne drops behind enemy lines. Paratroopers of the newly formed First Allied Airborne Army consisting of two British, and three US divisions, plus a Polish brigade, would drop out of the sky and secure both ends of the major bridges at Eindhoven, Nijmegen and Arnhem.

Part two was Garden. This called for the British XXX Corp under General Horrocks to punch through the German lines from Antwerp relieving the hopelessly outnumbered airborne troops at each bridge as they went. Ron was one of 9,000 Sappers who were assigned the task of re-building bridges, or placing temporary ones as necessary to maintain the missions forward thrust.

Ron's job included clearing bridges over the Albert, and Escaut canals, and the Meuse (Maas) River. This was all very dangerous work, sometimes doing underwater demolition, more often than not under fire from enemy artillery. He remembers working in conditions where he could not see a darn thing and all the while feeling the vibrations of enemy shells landing on and around the bridges. He was scared stiff but once again grateful for the seriousness in which he had done his training.

Operation Market-Garden, though it did achieve many of its objectives was considered a failure for many reasons. The movie *A Bridge Too Far* does a better than average job of documenting this action that lasted from September 17th to 25th. The mission failed to secure the last bridge at Arnhem where the 1st Airborne Division held with its remaining 700 men a position that was estimated to need 10,000 reinforcements to hold it. They were eventually and inevitably overrun. Their leader Lt. Colonel John Frost was wounded and captured.

One of the prisoners taken at Arnhem, Ken Hall, a veteran of five jumps behind enemy lines would many years later become the second husband of Ron's youngest sister Daphne in Canada.

The Allies had failed to cross the Rhine in sufficient numbers to hold their positions, dashing any hope of ending the war by Christmas 1944, which had been the prime objective of Market-Garden.

After Market-Garden, Ron's section with XXX Corp was moved back to Gent in Belgium for a four-day rest. He stayed at what he described as a beautiful 7th century Abby. It would have to have been either The Abby of Saint Peter or the Saint-Bavo Cathedral. We are not sure which. He remembers food being scarce everywhere both for the military and for civilians, and he often went out foraging from other army units for food to share with comrades and the locals

The next move was to S-Hertogenbosch in Holland. Ron would never forget this town, as it was here that twelve of his mates were killed when an ammunition dump that they were working on to remove booby-traps blew sky high. No one will ever know exactly what caused the detonation. It was war.

31. The Battle of The Ardennes

(The Battle of the Bulge).

From S-Hertogenbosch, Ron went to Helmond where he was working when on Dec 16th the Germans mounted their last and mightiest counter attack.

The Battle for the Ardennes which was mounted from Luxemburg through the Ardennes forest, involved three German armies which had the objective of breaking through to the coast, re-taking Brussels, the port of Antwerp and cutting the Allied forces in half. It was a daring, desperate attempt to keep the war out of Germany. They had surprise going for them and the winter weather. Overcast skies grounded the RAF.

There are a couple of good movies that describe this battle, *Band of Brothers* which is excellent in so many ways, and *The Battle of the Bulge,* which if you ignore the wimpy lieutenant played by MacArthur who would not have survived West Point let alone D-Day. Both of these place overwhelming emphasis on the siege of Bastogne. Heroic though it was for the US 101st who refused to surrender to a hugely superior force, and George Patton's amazing force march and wide swing to relieve, there were other more strategic facets to the defeat of this German offensive.

Never one to give Montgomery a lot of credit, in this battle he led the US 1st Army, and its ability to hold the German attack in the North really was the key to stopping the charge. It was this that allowed time for the US 3rd under Patton to join the fight and seal the defeat of the German initiative. In the end though, the Germans literally ran out of gas. They had to abandon their stranded tanks and walk home. Amazingly, the 7th Army once again battled to avoided annihilation and retreated to the Westwall, aka The Siegfried Line.

32. Winter: Muck and Bullits.

For the rest of 1944 and into 1945 the Second Army was occupied exploiting the salient that it had been created in the German line: controlling the Maas river, relieving all the Dutch territory and closing in on the Rhine itself.

By mid January they had cleared an area called The Roermond Triangle and completed the advance to the River Roer. Though not as well documented as some of the others we have mentioned, these were tough fought battles from hedge to hedge, village to village. Operation Blackcock was a complete success ending on Jan 26th.

The winter in Europe was one of the coldest on record. When they were not ducking for cover from bombardments of various kinds, they were freezing their nuts off.

Ron found spare duty as a dispatch rider. He liked motorbikes and it gave a break from his other routine. Riding along a dyke, he heard this loud ping sound and looking down saw that his knee was leaking. He had been hit by a sniper's bullet. I guess it was one more of his nine lives, as those people rarely missed their targets; Ron put it down to the fact his bike was bouncing up and down on extremely rough terrain. Anyway, this incident bought him a couple of days R&R in a Field Hospital. It was there on one particularly cold February afternoon when the first mail since late October arrived from home. Communication from home had been really awful because the troops were constantly on the move and in spite of the conscientious hard work done by amongst others, the Salvation Army, letters from home for anybody were few and very far between. Speaking of the 'Sally Ann' Ron would respect and support them for the rest of his life for their unselfish devotion to the spiritual and physical well being of all soldiers no matter what their nationality or religious stripe.

Ron opened and read several letters from Nellie in the order in which they had been written so as not to jump any guns. He came to the one dated November 11, 1944 in which he found out that he had a two-day-old son. Not wanting to dwell on the unthinkable but since Nellie had not heard from him for several months she called their son Ronald, just in case. Ronald was born at the general hospital in the beautiful cathedral town of Cobh and was baptized in the splendid cathedral itself.

Nellie was living with her mother in a block of tenement houses that formed a square. St, Patrick's Square by name. There were maybe six homes on each of the four sides and one entrance to the square. In the middle of all these houses was a green park.

Ron was tickled pink with the news that not only was his wife and daughter well and safe, he now also had a son to go home to. But he was also well aware that there was still work to do before he could go home to a safe Britain.

While Nellie was convalescing after childbirth and an attack of Phlebitis, her mother passed away. She only saw her new grandson the one time.

33. Crossing the Rhine: the death camp.

With the winter behind them, 96 Section with the 2nd Army was once more on the move. Their job during February had been to hold and pin down the German armies facing them while the Canadian 1st Army swung around from the north and the US 9th Army advanced from the south smashing through the Siegfried Line and clearing out all enemy forces west of the Rhine.

March 21st - Now the Rhine had to be crossed in the north with many bridges having been blown by the retreating army. Ron's job was building and installing Bailey Bridges. These amazing pieces of engineering went together like LEGO. All very straightforward unless you were being shelled bombed or strafed. The Royal Engineers took heavy casualties in this vital campaign called Operation Plunder. Ron crossed the Rhine on the March 23rd with the Second Army still flanked by the Canadians and the US. They trapped the German Army Group B in an enormous pocket in the Ruhr valley. This action essentially meant the end of the enemy in the west. The remnants retreated towards Berlin.

Ron's unit now attached to the British 11th Armoured Division proceeded up into northern Germany. It was on this leg of the campaign, on the route from Hannover to Hamburg that they liberated the 'Death Camp' at Bergen-Belsen on April 15th.

The sights that Ron witnessed were literally indescribable in their horror. He tells of mass graves with bodies six deep that had been left open by the enemy in their haste to retreat. There were people, men women and children wondering around, some naked, not knowing what the hell was going on. They just stared through hollow eyes at the soldiers unable to comprehend their deliverance. For any that doubt the existence of the holocaust be assured – it did take place.

Ron brought home an odd reminder of the camp. It was a flail comprised of a handle about 14" long with several leather thongs attached to one end. The thongs were about 17" long. This macabre object lay around our house for years. I remember one day not having seen it for a while, asking about it. My mother said she burned it, as she just could not live with it in her house any longer.

Ron's unit continued to go wherever they were needed and never it seems was their progress in a straight line. They went forwards sideways and back again depending on what and where obstacles presented themselves to the advancing armies.

34. THE WAR IS OVER.

They passed through the obliterated city of Bremen that paid a terrible price for its stiff resistance, crossing the Weser, Elbe Rivers. They then pushed through to Lubeck on the Baltic Sea and back down again to Hamburg that had capitulated on May 3rd.

A couple of days later, Ron was clearing underwater explosives from the North Sea harbour of Cuxhaven, famous as the home of the German U-Boats, and for the launching silos for the V2 rockets, when he got all tangled up under water, lost his air supply and had to do an emergency surface. The result was a blown eardrum that ended his diving career on May 5th, 1945. Two days later Germany surrendered. I mean how close was that? I suppose there are a lot of people who think back to those last few days and think what if? Can you imagine after surviving right through the war being killed on the day before the war ended? Sadly, many had been.

Attacking from the east, the Russians were the first troops to enter Berlin. Ron did not have a very high impression of them. He said the ones he encountered were very primitive and content to live in utter squalor. They had no concept of indoor plumbing and used the bathtubs as toilets.

One incident that Ron rarely spoke of occurred at the end of the war in the Berlin suburbs. He was foraging for food, as it seemed they so often were, when he heard a scream coming from a building. He investigated and came across two Russian soldiers one of whom was in the process of raping a young girl. He ordered them to stop but they thought it was a huge joke and just laughed at him - indicating that he should wait his turn.

One of the things Ron had acquired on his long campaign was a German 9mm Lugar that up to this point had only been used for target practice and the occasional rabbit. He now drew the gun from his belt to add weight to his demand for them to stop what they were doing, at which both soldiers went for their weapons. It was over in a flash, though he would have to live with it for the rest of his life. God knows why but it really bothered him. He untied the girl, found her clothes, handed them to her, consoled her as best he could but left quickly before any of their comrades arrived.

Ron's unit had been front line troops for virtually the whole eleven months since D-Day, and his section was given the honour of being part of the first British troop contingents to enter the City of Berlin. A memorable occasion to be sure. He could not believe the destruction.

The battle for Berlin in which he personally had no part, must have been something else. It seemed there was not a building left standing – really, not one. He had seen London in the Blitz, and had heard stories of the destruction of Coventry and Dresden, but nothing he had seen or heard of prepared him for Berlin. The tragedy is, that the war was lost absolutely by March of 1945. This was now into May. Hitler's hate and disdain for his own people for having in his estimation let him down, caused him, in his decent into total madness, to insist on continuing the resistance using children, old men, in fact anyone that could be pressed into service. Thousands of civilians, and soldiers died for nothing during those two months.

The war was over. Ron, both eardrums perforated, and a smashed right knee, accepted a honourable discharge. He would often reflect that his hatred of what the Nazi's stood for did not diminish his respect for the German soldier. If, God forbid, there should ever be a future conflict, he hoped to hell that they would be on the same side.

35. Winning the Peace.

He had survived. The war of course had a profound effect on him. He had watched his buddy make the supreme sacrifice by throwing himself onto a disturbed land mine in order to protect Ron and the rest of his team. He had lost so many friends and comrades. In fact none of his original mates survived. He would proudly march side by side with these men every November 11th for the rest of his life. As would his son for the rest of his.

Unlike some who returned from the war thinking that their country owed them something, on the contrary, Ron believed that he owed his country. He owed all those who did not return to their families. He would never ever accept that they might have died for nothing. He felt a deep-rooted obligation to try to make his world a better place for the families of the fallen, and those who would follow. He was a *'Private Ryan'* as in the novel and film. Ron was so indebted that if you can imagine, he refused to apply for a war pension until long after he retired many years later, as he felt others were more deserving. Don't ask.

Happy to be reunited in Cobh with his Nellie and their two children he was however bitterly disappointed that there was no housing available for them in his beloved Cuckfield. He had kept up correspondence with his mate Bonny's sister Kitty, who was now married and lived on a farm near the tiny hamlet of Four Marks in Hampshire, the county just west of Sussex. She offered a roof to the family until they could get organized. So over the four of them came from Ireland and moved in with Kitty and Walter.

36. Down on the farm: the simple life.

The farm was a most wondrous place. It is the source of my very earliest recollections. Amazingly, I returned many years later and the layout of the farmhouse; yards and milking sheds were totally familiar to me.

The industrial revolution had not yet reached this dairy farm. Every morning Uncle Walter would go out into the fields and call the cows that would obediently stroll single file out through the opened gate and into their own personal stall to be milked.

Walter would approach each animal with his small, low, three legged stool and after washing the udders with a cloth dipped in warm water, would proceed to milk each cow. This was done by grabbing the teats, two in each hand, squeezing and simultaneously pulling on them. This caused the fresh warm milk to squirt into the galvanized bucket making a very distinctive sound. The semi-feral farm cats would gather to salvage any spare drips, or on occasion Walter would give a cat a squirt much to the delight of the receiver and this chuckling little observer.

The ploughing, harvesting, and all farmland transportation were achieved using either one, or sometimes a team of two carthorses. These were immense beasts and once hitched up to a wagon, Walter would sit me on the back of one and let me believe that I was riding and controlling them. To this day, I love the smells of farmyards whether it is cows, horses, or pigs – but I do draw the line at chickens. They just stink.

Soon Dad got a job working at the local railway station, plus he did some chauffeuring, driving an old Packard automobile for a local landowner who afforded him the cheap use of a tithed cottage.

The family finally had its own place. And some place it was - no electricity, no heating, no running water, no inside plumbing – lots of vermin. An enormous coal or wood-burning stove served as both warmth provider and cooker. Mum kept a large urn of water on it at all times to supply hot water for all needs. Once a week the enormous tin bathtub would be placed in the middle of the kitchen floor and slowly filled with hot water, heated a pot at a time on the stove. This process was a battle of attrition as it took so long to heat the water that the preceding pot full was at best tepid by the time it was added to. It was all accomplished in the shadowed light from oil burning lamps or candles. These would also light our way up the rickety stairs to the frosted winter bedrooms. Mum would place bricks on top of the stove so she could wrap them in sacking to use as 'hot water bottles'. I suppose it helped but even so, we could not only still see our breath as it left our mouths but there was just as much frost on the inside of the windows as there was on the outside. Every bed had the obligatory potty under it, as a trip to the outhouse, in the dead of night, in the winter was a venture not to be undertaken lightly.

Our water came from a deep hole in the garden – a well. The closest nod to a modern convenience was that we had a hand pump in the kitchen connected to another well under the house. Hard to imagine that I learned how to prime a pump at that tender age, never mind checking the rat and mouse traps each morning and emptying the contents into a bucket of water in case there was still life.

Oddly, as hard as these experiences may have appeared at the time, in retrospect, these were wonderful days. I remember warm summers playing with my older sister Sheila making daisy chains in the fields by our cottage. Sheila was my princess and I was her prince. We both feared the 'mad driver' a man that sped through the fields in a lorry. He was, I am sure, just a farm hand but in our imaginations he was a very bad person and we had to protect each other from his evil.

This still being just a few years after the war, there seemed to be lots of convoys of military vehicles on the roads. We would watch their seemingly endless parades going past our garden gate. I built my own roads in the garden and populated them with imaginary cars;

tanks and trucks simulated by the use of any object, from a matchbox to a package of Tide. And heaven help anyone who disturbed my roads. Of course, Sheila did, and got paid back on one occasion by my peeing into her Wellington boot – she never would wear them again. In fact, she need not have taken it so personally as I apparently had a penchant for peeing everywhere, anywhere, and in anything. There being no flush toilets, and my not being uncouth enough to just hang it out just anywhere, I instead chose bottles, cans, and yes even my sister's gumboots. It was only my mother's warning that one of these days I would get my Willie stuck in a bottle that slowed this practice.

Madge, Theresa, Matty, Nancy, Mum (and Ellen, in background).

These were, as I say, days of utter contentment for us children. Then the day came when Sheila went off to school. Oh boy, I was devastated. It was the cause of my first great sadness but only to have it dissipated when she leapt into my arms on her return each day, and we would walk together arm in arm up the long pathway from the gate to the cottage like a pair of young lovers.

The farm cottage at this time seemed to have a somewhat permanent parade of houseguests. Nellie, as had Dad, came from a family of seven children. She was the oldest. Her brothers, Isaac who would immigrate to Australia in the late 40s, and Matty who like Mum, would also end up in Cuckfield. The girls were Nancy, Madge, Theresa, and Mary. Theresa, a lively, redheaded bundle of energy, came to stay with us for a while before moving on to a job in London and brother Matty also stayed with us when he came over from Ireland to find work.

Then came Ellen, our new sister who just seemed to arrive without notice. The initial excitement soon paled to the incessant noise of her crying, and our need to be quiet all the time. What a pain new sisters are. Gosh when I do think back at what our mother had to contend with. Living in that place: a husband, two children under six, two adult relatives, and a new baby. It must have been quite a challenge. In terms of income, to say she lived on nothing is pretty close to the mark. Dad worked long hours, at two jobs, for very little pay.

I know they discussed emigrating to one of the 'New Worlds', in fact Dad was made some pretty enticing offers to go to South Africa as a deep sea diving consultant. Mum would have gone in the bat of an eye but Dad was much more cautious, plus, he felt this overwhelming duty to help rebuild England.

37. BACK TO CUCKFIELD.

One of my earliest recollections is taking a ride on a railway train with just my mother; the reason for the trip escapes me. Mum had this odd expression when exasperated with us, or pressed with too many questions about what she was doing and where she was going, she would simply say that she is going to run away with a black man. In England at this time, there were so few people that were not Caucasian, in fact, I had never even seen one. So low and behold at the very first stop the train made, into our crowded compartment came this enormous GI and yep you guessed it – he was black. In the loudest whisper ever known to man I asked my Mum if this was the black man she kept running away with. Mum was mortified.

Dad could not wait to get back to Cuckfield. For a man who had only a very basic education and had gotten most of his learning from being a consummate reader, he was an excellent writer. He used this skill in petitioning the Member of Parliament for Mid-Sussex and local land baron, a Colonel Clarke, to get him back home to Cuckfield.

After the war the governments went into a home-building frenzy in part to provide jobs, and for an even larger part to provide homes for the million or so men at arms who had left England as boys and returned as grown men, many now with families.

The prime addition to the village of Cuckfield in terms of new Council Housing was a subdivision called Brainsmead. Persistent letter writing finally paid off for Dad, in the summer of 1948, the family was loaded onto a lorry, leaving Hampshire for the long journey to 11 Brainsmead Road, a million miles away. As the truck bumped down the yet unpaved road to number 11, you could smell the sand, bricks, and cement of a building site. It was all so new. Ours was one of the first houses to be completed. It was at the far end of the road, and the end of a fourplex.

The truck came to a stop and we threw back the tarp that served as a back door to the moving-lorry and were greeted by a curious brother and sister, two shy and very blonde-haired children, Peter and Jill. They looked like little angels. The first game we played was trying to guess each other's names. I was not very good at it, as I had never had playmates before other than Sheila so I quickly ran out of guesses. Peter was a bit better than a year older than me, and Jill was younger, they lived at the other end of the fourplex. I think I appeared a bit wild to them. I just did not know how to interact with other children. Soon a set of twin boys Martin and Barry with their younger brother Ian moved in next-door and the gang was formed. They, Peter, a second Ian from around the corner in Brainsmead Close, Vanessa from the Ship Inn Pub, the one-eyed Anthony also from the fourplex and Sheila and me were the 'Brainsmead Gang'. Anthony had a special trick he would do at the drop of a hat – he would pop his false eye out – really. I wanted one. His older brother Kenny had curly hair – I wanted that too, so Mum put my hair in curlers for a few nights. They were awfully uncomfortable so I settled for eating my bread crusts, which Dad said would have the same effect.

Mum was in heaven. Can you imagine the contrast between what she had just left and what she now would call her home – forever. The door had a lock (not that it was ever used, in my memory), the lights went on with just the flick of a switch, there was a boiler in the corner of the kitchen that heated radiators in every room in the house, water just ran out of a tap when you turned it on – hot and cold! She also had a beautiful spanking new electric stove. The building was critter-tight plus the view from the northeast facing windows was to die for – uninterrupted vistas of the Sussex Wield from Cuckfield down through the valleys and up again to the beginning of the Forrest Ridge at Balcome. It is no small wonder that this place became, and lived on in all our memories as a magical dwelling.

There were three bedrooms, one for Mum and Dad and baby Ellen, one for me and Mum's brother Matty, and one shared by Sheila and Mum's sister Mary. Mary was Mum's second youngest sister, a tragic figure in so many ways. As a result of meningitis as a child, she was blind and quite crippled plus she had an arm amputated above the wrist. Our mother had been pressed into giving their mother a deathbed promise to always look after Mary. A bright young girl trapped by fate in this dilapidated body. It all seemed so unfair. We grew up with her. She took us to bed each night with a 'sweetie' and said our prayers with us. For many years, the last thing on my prayer list was for Aunty Mary to see again. I was very disappointed with God for this. It was not going to happen and sadly, Mary just sat and declined in body and spirit. There were really no services to help in those days. She had someone come by every now and then and try to get her to weave baskets. She hated it. I think she was smart enough to be intellectually insulted that this was all she was deemed good for. After many years living with Mum, she returned to Ireland and eventually passed away in a care home. I did get to see her once more at the home, during a trip to Ireland, it was very upsetting.

38. SETTLING IN AND GROWING UP.

Dad meantime had hooked up with his cousin Arthur Knight (the Knight part was no direct relation, a female cousin on his mother's side just happened to also marry a man with the name Knight and Arthur was a result). Interestingly though, through a strenuous gene on the Botting side of the family, Dad and Arthur did bare a strong family resemblance. Anyway, Arthur had his own window-cleaning business and more houses in his 'book' then he could reasonably service, so he sold a route to Dad, mostly those in and around Cuckfield. He also sold Dad a bicycle with a sidecar for holding ladders.

Let me tell you it was bloody hard work pedaling that damn bike up hill and down dale with the weight of the ladders. At times it was all you could handle to keep the forward motion going in any kind of a straight line. The work itself was also very hard, out in all temperatures he seemed to be either sweating his balls off or breaking the ice on his bucket to finish a windowpane before the moisture froze on it.

The amount of money he felt he could reasonably charge for his window cleaning services did not add up to a decent wage so he opted to augment his income with a full-time job at the local dairy. At Gubbins' Dairy, he delivered milk door to door from 4:00 am till just after noon six days a week. He went home for lunch and then went out cleaning windows till five or six at night. Long days. We never heard him complain though and in fact I think he was quite content. He was home in his much-loved village and his family was well fed. In fact, though we were all aware that there was no spare money, we never lacked for food, warmth, or love.

My parents never had a bank account, there was no need of one - there was never anything to put in it. Mum was the 'banker'. She had eggcups in the kitchen cupboard that were earmarked for various necessities. Dad gave her all his earnings and she would plot out the family budgets by collecting coins in eggcups for things like rent, coal, and any other vital need.

Dad might have done a lot better financially if it were not for the fact he was always doing favours for his customers. He would do grocery shopping for people and deliver them as he did his milk rounds. He would pick fruit from trees belonging to old ladies', dig their gardens, mend their sash-cord windows, mow their lawns – all this for no financial compensation other than perhaps a bag of apples or pears.

Brainsmead was good to us all though. As children, we would roam for miles around, probably only within a four-mile radius but in fact, that covered a lot of territory. The countryside was our playground - the woods, fields, and streams. We learned to socialize, cooperate, respect nature, and other people's property. We built forts, camps, and tree houses. We dammed brooks to create small swimming holes. We swung from trees, scrumped fruit, and nestled in the hay-bails of barn lofts. There were cold days huddled around campfires smoking nicked fags (Weights and Woodbines), and warm lazy summer afternoons sun-bathing beside a lake or stream.

We collected birds' eggs, carefully pricking both ends and blowing the yolks out so the shell would keep. Collecting eggs from the nest of birds such as swans and carrion crows was no easy task. The safest way to transport an egg was to put it in one's mouth, leaving both hands free to climb. One time, having risked life and limb retrieving a rook's egg from the spindly upper branches of an enormous elm tree and egg in mouth, I dropped the last six feet to the ground and . . . yep!

39. OFF TO SCHOOL: THE CONVENT.

During this time, of course I began my school days, starting at kindergarten. Off I went on my 'brand new' second-hand bike, along with my sister Sheila to Mount St. Joseph's Convent in Hayward's Heath. This was the closest Catholic school to us in the area. It was in a nearby town about two and a half miles from home. This, my first day, was all very exciting. Beginning with riding on the main roads on my little bike, my lunch packed in my leather school satchel, bouncing on my back. I felt very grown-up for a four – going on five-year old, resplendent in my neat school uniform.

As the name convent implies, nuns ran the school – very scary creatures to a little boy in their stark and heavily starched black and white habits with shiny, buckled, shoes.

My first teacher was a beautiful nun by the name of Sister Stanislaus and I was smitten for the first time in my young life. Women have always been my weakness and at times downfall, and Sister Stanislaus was to be the very first of many wonderful infatuations. She had the softest speaking voice with just a faint hint of an Irish accent; it was as if she were purring. She was graceful and in her uniform that almost touched the ground, she seemed to actually float across a room. I tried hard to please her and therefore actually learned well in my first year, unfortunately the next three – not so much. The second year teacher was a lay-teacher by the name of Miss Keeping, and man what a battle-axe she turned out to be. I believe she was a sister of the Reverend Mother and school principal. Not that that mattered in itself, it was just that she was on a real crusade on behalf of discipline for what seemed like discipline's sake. We did not hit it off, subjecting to discipline never being my strong suit. I think perhaps because of the semi-solitude of my formative years, I had acquired a strong need for independent action, thought, and expression none of which were appreciated in Miss Keeping's classroom. The outcome was a regular daily assault on my person with a 24" ruler that she could wield with equal dexterity with either hand, and target hand or bum – flat or on edge.

In part to redeem my immortal soul, I enrolled as an Altar Boy and took the necessary lessons from the assistant priest at the St. Paul's Parish Church. Fortunately, we did not have to go all the way to

Hayward's Heath every Sunday for Mass as there was a conveniently placed small chapel attached to Cuckfield Hospital, a mere two fields away reached by way of a footpath. We were all herded along, rain, sleet, or snow to Sunday morning Mass, a ritual that none of us ever dared miss on pain of, if not divine intervention, then at the very least the incurrence of Mum's wrath. It was at this chapel that I served as an Altar Boy. I must admit though it was to show off in front of the local crumpet that yielded the most attraction for me. I wore my Sunday best though my person was mostly covered up with a black full length dress-like Cotter over which was worn a starched white Surplus. All very swish and it was my ardent hope that this, and my clear, perfect Latin, would not go unnoticed by my favourite parishioner, the delectable Miss Ponsford. Unfortunately it was. She was from a quite wealthy farming family and looking to be even wealthier, bless her. I was not considered a likely candidate on that career path. I believe Miss Ponsford went on to marry a member of the ultra rich 'Hayward Pickle' family.

Fortunately my year with Miss Keeping was soon over and I moved up and away from this brute of a woman who as far as I know never left the second year kindergarten, I guess she just preferred to beat up little kids, or so it seemed to me.

One thing that sticks out in my mind was the horrible day that Sheila, while trying to fish out her satchel that had been thrown into a bramble bush by some kid, scratched her iris. She needed stitches in her eye to fix the problem and never had complete use of that eye. It was very scary.

40. Diagnosed as having had Polio.

For the next couple of years the beatings were no less brutal but perhaps a little less regular. It was during this period that my Mum after many attempts to get a doctors attention regarding the malformation of my right leg, was finally successful in getting us in to see an orthopedic specialist, and arriving at a diagnoses of sorts. It seems that while back in Hampshire I had a 'unaccounted for illness' in which I had an alarmingly high temperature and sleeping sickness for a period of two weeks. I recovered from this malaise and seemed to be just fine. The consensus now seemed to be that I had contracted Infantile Paralyses – Polio. I got this in all probability from drinking the well water that drew from the same vicinity in which we disposed of our waste.

The result of this disease manifested itself in my right leg that lacked strength, started to look wasted, and produced in me a slight limp. Kids being kids and cruel little bastards, I was the subject of name calling, and often just left behind when we were out playing, hiking, or out on our bikes. I was a good size for my age and could hold my own in a scrap with most kids that I associated with but this was hard to fight. I wanted to be up front – a leader, and popular. The gimp at the back did not quite qualify.

Once a week, Mum took me to a clinic in the small nearby town of Burgess Hill. When I say nearby, it was only five miles, but without our own transportation, other than bikes, and Mum never did ride one, we had to take a half hour bus-ride to the station, wait for a train, and from the station at the other end, walk for 45 minutes to the clinic. It took all day to get a half hour's physiotherapy. Was it worth it? Well I guess so. I know both Mum and Dad really worked hard at it, putting me on the kitchen table every night before bed and stretching out my leg's muscles and tendons. The doctors had painted a bleak picture of my physical potential but my parents refused to accept their view, and not only never gave up themselves, they never let me quit or make excuses for lack of effort. Excelling was not the issue but giving it my best shot at all times was. They encouraged me to take part in all sports, which I did. Dad was a super-jock and I am sure I was a bit of a disappointment to him but if I was he never let on. I got into high jump, swimming, and table tennis, boxed a little, and played in goal at football.

41. An Irish Wedding.

To say money was tight is a huge understatement. We had no car, no phones certainly no TV. We still had no bank account. Mum's eggcups were as busy as ever. The rent was always the first to be fed, and in the cold months she also had one for fuel – coke and coal, and a spare in which she saved for all other needed items such as shoes and clothes for us children. Most of our clothes were either bought at 'Jumble Sales' or Mum made them. There was no such thing as pocket money or allowances; we did however get a treat every Saturday morning. It was called the ABC Minors at the Paramount cinema in Hayward's Heath. Mum gave us sixpence to get into the theatre, two three-penny bits for the bus, and three pence for an ice cream. I used to skip the ice cream and thumb a ride home in order to save sixpence a week. This was the closest thing we ever got in the way of an allowance or pocket money.

The movies were great, we had: cartoons, White Eagle was my favourite cowboy, and then there was Dick Tracy in which the bad guys always scared the shit out of me when they showed up. Of course we would play-act the shows we had just seen, on the bus all the way home which was another reason I most often thumbed home because I rarely made it all the way anyway before the conductor threw me off.

From my little savings, I had enough money put away for Uncle Matt to take me with him to Ireland to attend his marriage to Aunty Ethel. This was a great adventure. We went from Hayward's Heath by train to London, across London on a bus from Victoria Station to Paddington, there to board another train for the five-hour trip to the southwest tip of Wales. From Fishguard we took the overnight boat ride on the good ship Innisfallen, an aging tramp steamer that plied between Wales and Cork Harbour in southern Ireland. Man, what a crossing that was. Getting some fresh air on deck, and looking forward, one minute I was looking straight up at the sky only to be faced with a solid wall of green water the next. It seemed like everyone aboard was sick and of course we had no private cabins so we cat-napped huddled in hallways that stank of vomit, for the seven long hours.

In the morning, as we entered the second largest natural harbour in the world (next to Sydney, Australia), the sea was as calm as in the night it was rough. The slow trip through the beautiful harbour and way up the inlet to the docks at Cork City was wonderful.

As we passed our home town of Cobh with its magnificent and dominant St. Coleman's Cathedral where I had been baptized, dozens of small water craft buzzed out to great the ship, along with a Tender that picked up mail and other deliveries from England. It really was all so wondrous.

The wedding was great, especially for my cousin Vintone and me. At least it was once we got the interminable ceremony, and the hour and a half Nuptial Mass with communion out of the way. We sat together on the floor just about under the beer barrel and caught drips as each person filled their mugs and moved away. It was my first family wedding and an Irish wedding at that. There would seem to be a certain pattern to these events. First, they drink, then they sing and dance, and then they fight, only to start the whole programme over again.

42. END OF THE CONVENT: EXPELLED (1952).

Shortly after my return from the wedding, came that fateful day at school. Things had not been going too well for me. On reflection, I certainly had what they would call today 'Attention Deficit Disorder' (at the very least) plus, though I would not discover this until way into my 40s, I had a form of dyslexia. I read words correctly but my written words were all over the place. Spell-check was forty years away and as my wife would one day so eloquently put it. "In order for spell-check to be of assistance, one has to be close, and for those that consistently fail to distinguish between the likes of beer, bear and bare – there is no hope". Anyway it did not help my cause that I also developed a penchant for being the class clown. I think I was bright enough but thought I should be leading the class, not partaking of it. Due to the disruptions I caused, they had me sent up a class for a while to see if that would help my behaviour. When that did not work, they sent me down a class to perhaps humiliate me into behaviour more conducive to peace in the classroom. All very confusing.

Well this particular day we were going to play football (soccer), and off we all went on a pathway that meandered from the school buildings through some lovely woods, to the football pitch. The teacher leading this group of boys was a very good looking young woman whom, to keep the attention of her charges who varied in age from about seven to ten years, until they reached the field, used the surroundings that were indeed reminiscent of Sherwood Forest of folklore, to her advantage by play-acting the story of Robin Hood.

Now this would have been all very fine if I could have been cast as Robin to her Marion, however that role was ceded to one of the ten-year olds while I was relegated to playing one of the not so merry men. Sorry, but that is just not where I saw myself. We reached the football field before the key participants were ready to relinquish their fantasies, and after several minutes which seemed like forever I went up to my vision of ethereal loveliness and told her to 'blow her bloody whistle and let's get on with the game'. She turned me in. I spent the rest of the day in solitary confinement, still in my prize leather and heavily dubbin'd football boots, in the convent chapel supposedly in contemplation of, and penance for, my sins. I was then sent home with the note calling for a teacher-parent consultation.

Oh boy, this could not be good. Mum cried and prayed for some kind of exorcism to intervene, Dad did his best to calm her down.

My parents completed their humiliation by being kept waiting for half an hour before being told that I was totally out of control and perhaps would be better served in a school that had male teachers to keep me in line. That was it – expelled at the tender age of eight. Poor Mum. She was a truly devout Catholic encompassing all that that entailed. She unquestioningly followed the doctrine of the church, which could do no wrong. Blinders, to some, to her it were unshakable faith. Now her only son was not only unlikely to be a priest, but was bordering on excommunication. The resulting family conflab was very emotional on Mum's part. This caused me a great deal of anguish as I did, and always would take pain with her pain. Dad, ever the consolatory voice of calm and reason told me that I would have to go down to the Cuckfield village school in the morning and enroll in the state-run school.

43. Cuckfield Primary School.

That was that. Up early, off I went, all on my own down to the century's old Cuckfield village public school to enroll. I arrived and asked at the reception to be directed to the head master, a Mr. Schwartz who interviewed me and confused me by constantly referring to me as 'Sir'. I was a polite boy if you didn't tick me off, and in between my many aforementioned shortcomings knew how to behave in public, so I answered all his questions followed by the word 'Sir'. He did the same darn thing, very confusing I did not know if he was taking the piss or what, but anyway it seemed that I was now enrolled. I had apprised him of my mother's directive that I would not partake in his heathen prayers or religious instruction, it being a Protestant school. This was acceptable to Mr. Schwartz who assured me they would find some suitable studious endeavours for me to attend in order to occupy my time. This was also in all likelihood my first encounter with discrimination, prejudice, and bigotry.

I and one other child were the only Catholics in the school and were very obviously singled out for 'special' treatment. It is hard to understand why our Church would be so paranoid as to think that being exposed to prayers at 'assembly' would corrupt my spirituality but such was the case in the Catholic realm. We were actually forbidden to even enter a Protestant church. Anyway, this meant that every Monday morning, after the headmaster's announcements, I had to stand up and leave the assembly while the rest of the school continued with their supplications. The result of this was that my fellow students thought me different and though I oft shared this view, theirs was not in a nice way. All children have a need to fit in, and ridicule by peers is hard to deal with at any level.

Education-wise I think I did well at this school. The corporal punishment continued somewhat unabated, I got walloped a couple of times a week by my housemaster Mr. Evens. His favourite target was the back of the legs above my long socks and below my shorts. It hurt like hell. I then had to try to hide the welts from my parents or I would be in further trouble from them! It all became a predictable pattern, and for the most part tolerable.

I was the top student of every class I was in, and other than my dyslexic approach to spelling, I even excelled in English. Words were music to me and I stretched my vocabulary to its limit at every opportunity whether I spelled correctly or not. I would prefer to include an interesting word and risk the spelling then let my essay be dull. I still do.

In spite of his bad temper and his brutality, Mr. Evens was a good instructor. He read to us in such a way that we looked forward to the next chapter that would come the following day. He had a voice for each character that helped keep our interest and attention, and if that failed a piece of flying chalk or on one occasion the tri-podded blackboard seemed to work.

44. Family get-togethers at Number 11.

Our family was all musically inclined. Just about everyone played at least one instrument even if it was only a comb with a piece of toilet paper wrapped round it, which when blown through gave a sound like a kazoo. We had piano, accordion, mouth organ, jew's-harp, and spoons. And everybody sang. Parties at Number 11 Brainsmead were legendary.

Christmas, Easter, and birthdays in between, the family would gather. Mum would cook and bake for days to lay a fine table. After everybody had eaten his or her fill, the music would start. There was no record player in the house and the radio relied on a six-volt battery that always seemed to be dead, so we made our own music. It usually started with Uncle Mac who was married to our Aunty Theresa, either on the accordion or on the piano. He never read a note of music that I ever saw but if he could hum it, he could play it, with a very listenable touch on the keys. Each member of the family had their favourite song and Mac new them all, making sure that he got to all of them in turn. We would also play silly, active, parlour games like Squeak Piggy Squeak, Blind Man's Bluff, the Hokey Pokey, and the Rumba. They were great times though all the adults smoked like chimneys, which sent me eyes streaming from the room by mid-evening. After the party, the front room and the dining room became bedrooms for our family, while the guests used all our three bedrooms. Yes, it was the protocol that guests had the finest accommodation the house could offer.

The mouth organ was my favourite instrument while growing up. I had several harmonicas in various keys, plus my pride and joy, a Hohner Chronomatic. What made this mouth organ exceptional is that it gave me access to sharps and flats allowing me to play more complex tunes, and in different keys.

The interest in music prompted my parents to start an 'Eggcup bank' for my music lessons. When they had saved two shillings and sixpence, Dad would make an appointment for a piano lesson. He unleashed me on an unfortunate timid old-maid who gave lessons in her rather smelly front room that was impregnated with the aroma of old furniture, and un-house trained dogs. She was actually very sweet and did her best to impart the rudiments of music to me. The tunes of Tchaikovsky and Straus I found to be most inspiring. It was likely their subtle simplicity and strong melody lines that had appeal for me, as throughout my life I would gravitate to this type of music regardless of the genre. If there are too many notes making the tune hard to hum or whistle, I tend to tune out completely. Heavy classical and modern Jazz leave me in their dust. The gratitude I feel for having taken music lessons is immeasurable. Not that I ever became a pianist of any note, it was just that the bit of knowledge which penetrated my antsy metabolism set me up to love, appreciate and enjoy music in many forms throughout my life. I have oft joked that I could live without love but not without music.

45. THE WOODS WERE MY TEACHERS.

I cannot think of a nicer place to grow up then in the English countryside. Square mile after mile of woods, fields, rivers and hills. As children, we would wander abroad from dawn to dusk without any adult supervision, right from the age of four on. It was usually hunger that brought us home at day's end or sometimes, extreme cold. We often left the house with a packed lunch comprised of our favourite sandwich plus a piece of cake. Most days the repast was polished off in the first hour. Our wanderings on foot were in a radius of three to four miles and later on bicycles, up to twelve miles. We had our favourite destinations of course and I will reflect on a few that stand out so clearly in my memory.

Spring Valley – Only a few fields from our home, we gave it this name for the abundance of bluebells, daffodils and primroses that adorned this place in exactly that order each spring. The valley was no more than half a mile long and had steep sides falling down to an all year around spring. At its widest the valley was maybe one hundred feet. This place was perfect for swinging ropes from one side to the other, sliding down on one's backside, and for damming the stream thereby creating paddling pools. There was another valley that ran at a right angle to the end of this one, and the two together made for a terrific site for playing Snipers and Cowboys & Indians. I developed an affinity for the Redman even at this early age. He seemed such a noble underdog. I loved playing Geronimo, Cochise, and Crazy Horse.

The Bracken Fields – this long, wide banked area grew thick with ferns each year. These ferns or bracken were great for weaving the walls of our forts. The rolling banks were also the home to hundreds of rabbits, which we snared as youngsters, sometimes using ferrets to chase the animals from their burrows. As we got a little older, we used small-bore shotguns.

Building forts was a favourite pastime. We built them in trees, dug them underground, and perched them on ridges – and we stockpiled them with all sorts of ordinance: spears, bows & arrows staves, clubs – all in preparation for the inevitable attack by the dreaded Glebe Road Gang – that never came.

The River Ouse – This is one of three significant rivers that drain the County of Sussex. It has its source at Slaugham Place Mill Pond a historic little village near Handcross just off the M23 motorway. It meanders through the beautiful Sussex countryside to find its exit to the English Channel at the seaside resort of Newhaven. We would intercept this babbling brook at many places along its path. We fished in it for minnows and if lucky a small trout, we swam in it, and rafted it on logs. The river also ran under the Ouse Valley Viaduct, a train track running from London to Brighton, and spanning the valley for some four hundred and fifty yards at a height of over ninety feet. What a place to play this monument was. The ever-present danger of the fast moving trains and the electrified rails all added to the excitement of being there. My braver friends would walk the length of this bridge on an outside ledge no more than two-feet wide and lie down when a train came by, to avert the prospect of being shaken off and plunging to the river below. Never having an affinity for heights I would run the length on the inside and jump into a shallow recess put there for that purpose for when railway workers were on the viaduct. It was all very exciting. One neat trick was to put a penny on the rail and after a train had gone by, see if you could find this flattened disk. I have a photo taken with a Brownie Box camera, of a train barreling towards me as I stood in the tracks between the north and the south 'hot' rails. What makes this as silly as can be is that to direct this old classic camera you had to look straight down into the viewfinder and shade it with your other hand. Trust me, it makes it hard to tell how far away the eighty-mile an hour train is!

Then there was the Circle Woods, Cuckfield Park with its infestation of poisonous adders; The Recreation Ground, aka 'the Reck', with its secluded park benches, Blunt's Wood and the South Downs. All playgrounds to pretend in and explore, and I have to believe this was more fun and educational than today's children have just using their thumbs on a keypad.

Oh and did I mention all the hay filled barns dotted around the farmlands where we would play my favourite game – Doctors and Nurses.

One particular excursion stands out in my mind. We were swimming under the bridge that spans a river separating Cuckfield from Ansty, when one of us saw shiny objects among the rocks on the riverbed. By the time we were through, we had collected forty-eight bullets, twenty-one sticks of dynamite and . . . a Mortar Bomb. We took our haul home to my Dad, being careful not to mention the fact that we had been trying to set the bomb off by chucking rocks at it. Dad placed the stuff into a garbage can and carried it into the middle of a field by our house for the authorities to deal with. The story is that an army jeep went off the bridge during the war and nobody bothered to clear up the mess.

46. THE CUCKFIELD YOUTH CLUB.

The village church Curate in Cuckfield had asked Dad if he would help at the church boys' club. Apparently, some of the boys had expressed an interest in boxing and though not a member of his Protestant congregation, Dad's name had come up in conversation as someone who had some experience. The Curate, or assistant Vicar was an ultra-typical Church of England cleric, almost a caricature. A thoroughly decent little man, very quiet spoken and humble to the point of being constantly apologetic. He had started this boys' club as an extension of Sunday school, except that it was held one night a week, on Tuesdays. The boys that went to church with their parents on Sundays, also showed up on Tuesdays when the Curate had the church hall available for them to play table tennis, darts, chess, and billiards.

The first night Dad went down to observe, he took me with him. There were about a dozen or so boys ranging in age from eight to fourteen in attendance. It was all very organized. The Reverend had sign-up sheets for each activity and cooking timers to make sure that no one overstayed their time slots. It was too organized for Dad's liking. When the bell went off the activity stopped even if it was in the middle of a game. He also noted that there were several boys and some girls hanging around outside of the hall and when questioned by Dad the Curate told him they were just riff-raff troublemakers and he was frightened that they might cause problems in his club.

Well Dad gave this a lot of thought, it was just the sort of opportunity he had been looking for to subscribe to his payback mentality. He had been very involved with doing lots of stuff for the Convent school, assisting with Garden Fetes, Open Days, and that sort of thing but now that I was out of that school and Sheila was also now in a Secondary school in Crawley his ties to the Convent had loosened.

In his next meeting with the Curate Dad outlined his vision for the club. Firstly, as he had children of both sexes he did not want to spend such a great deal of his time at an endeavourer that did not include all his family, so the club would have to accommodate boys and girls. Secondly, it would have to be non-denominational. Although he had converted to Catholicism when he married Mum, he really was always a Christian first and being a member of any sect was a long second. Next, he wanted all children to be welcome regardless of background, reputation, religion, or sex. The young Curate with some trepidation accepted these terms and the Cuckfield Youth Club was born.

47. CHRISTINE AND ELIZABETH (1953).

Speaking of born, the next year, 1953 we were all surprised by the addition to the family of sister Christine. And I do mean surprised. Hard to imagine that a nine-year old would be oblivious to his mother's pregnancy but that kind of was the case right up to the last few weeks. I claim some responsibility for naming the child in that the reigning love of my life was a flaxen haired Dutch girl who's name was Christine and it seemed that anyone being given that name must end up special. She did. As our Christine was just a child when I would move out, I only got to know her as an adult, married to Ted Murphy and with three children: Michael, Leanne and Jo.

That lovely Dutch girl by the way had a gorgeous blue Triumph bicycle that lived with her way out in the country down Deaks Lane. I convinced my pals to ride over there many times with me in the hopes of getting a glimpse of her. She was the girl of my dreams. Unfortunately, no matter how I showed off in her presence, I did not exist in her world.

1953 was also the year of the coronation of Queen Elizabeth II. It would be another couple of years before we got our first 9" black & white TV but we were invited to a wealthy customer of Dad's to watch the big event on their massive 18" set. Afterwards we rushed back to Brainsmead to join the huge parade and street celebrations that were held in the Road. The families had been planning all year for this event. The Road was beautifully decorated with wooden arches across the street ornately covered with flowers, banners, and tree boughs. There was a fancy dress parade and competition in which parents and children enthusiastically participated. There were dozens of tables set up in the street for a fabulous potluck feast. We had musicians, jugglers, and clowns. It was a real high-class, even award winning event.

48. A TRUE COMMUNITY.

As I mentioned, TV had not yet really arrived in our strata of society. There was only one in our entire road at this time, and all us little kids were allowed to go to Mrs. Riddles' house to watch The Lone Ranger once a week. This was the evening highlight of our young lives. We poured out of her place to the strains of *The William Tell Overture*, all taking turns to play Tonto and the great man himself.

There is something very wonderful about a small community and the way people get involved with events. An example is Christmas. All the children would gather in the Queens Hall at the top of the town hill where there would be tables set out loaded with fancy food, all potluck. After the meal was over there would be entertainment: a magician perhaps, a clown, or just someone to get a sing-a-long going.

One year the main entertainment did not show up so I nipped home on my bike and returned with my stuff. I got up on stage and did a show that included playing tunes on my harmonica, doing a ventriloquist act and several magic tricks. The kids loved it and I felt very chuffed by the acknowledgment. It may have been my first public performance and whetted my appetite for applause. As the evening wore on, one parent set up a noisy clack, clack, clack, movie projector and we all watched 'A Christmas Carol' staring Alistair Simms as Scrooge. Scared the crap out of me. As we left the hall that night it was snowing like crazy and all the way home I expected Marley's ghost to jump out from behind every hedge waving his clanking chains.

One of the activities that Dad and Mum put a lot of time into was the preparation for Guy Fawkes Night. In England, November 5th was celebrated for the day that a thwarted plot to blow up the Houses of Parliament with King James I in it by a Catholic (what else) dissident named Guy Fawkes. He was tortured into confession, and sentenced to be hanged, drawn, and quartered. He would cheat this hideous fate by jumping from the scaffold, breaking his neck. Ever since, November 5th has been a day when people gather to recreate that almost fateful day by lighting bonfires, dressing up in costumes and setting off fireworks to emulate the Parliament going up in smoke. It is still a great temptation I must admit.

Brainsmead had an ad-hoc committee that organized the event for all the children. The parents would put some money away each week that would be used to buy fireworks. All the men with Dad being a key participant would meet to make torches to light the procession. These were comprised of a four-foot stick that was wound at one end with strips of sacking held in place with wire. These were then soaked for days in kerosene. The men would also organize the building of the bonfire on Whiteman's Green. Of course all us kids contributed by dragging trees, old tires – anything that needed disposing of, and would burn. The Mums made costumes out of old clothes, blankets, curtains, and sheets.

The festivities would start with all the children getting something to eat and then the local Brass Band would lead a torch-light procession of all the fancied dressed adults and children around the village ending up at the Green where all those with torches that were still burning, would light the bonfire. It was a super event. Dad would be both a participant and a 'bouncer' There were a few times that I saw him disarm ruffians who were throwing firecrackers into the crowd. He did not mess around. One time he was watching this bloke, and as he drew his arm back to hurl the squib, Dad just grabbed and held his elbow. The squib went off. Man, that must have hurt, but hey, there were little kids in the parade.

49. Vintone: 1955.

Around this time, I had another run-in with God. On a visit to Ireland, I had spent a lot of time with my cousin Vintone. He was an outgoing charmer of a lad and we got along very well. While on holiday, at his home in Cobh, the circus came to town and set up in the fields right behind his house, so naturally he and I gravitated to this thrilling venue. We watched, from the erecting of the first Big Top tent, right through to opening night. It was magical. We snuck into all the prohibited areas, checked out the animals, and watched the training and practices. The circus folk did not seem to mind a couple of curious scallywags nosing around. Of course in our imaginations we were part of the act and worked hard to out brag each other on our exploits. We flew through the air, tamed ferocious tigers, and got shot from cannons while all the time being heralded as some kind of hero runaways.

Less than a year later, our kitchen at home was the scene for the receipt of the tragic news that Vintone had died of Leukemia. I had never been visited by a death before and this was quite devastating. The anger that I felt was directed at the 'God of love' that we had all been taught had a great design for us all, and I just could not readily accept what possible purpose the taking of my pal's life could serve.

It is a most unfortunate facet of Catholic indoctrination that its disciples are so poorly equipped and educated to deal with questions regarding the Church and its faith other than the inadequate platitudes prescribed by quotes from the catechism. There are no answers, except that it is all to do with faith in the will of God. What ends up happening is that any hard question is dismissed as an affront to the belief in God for which the only punishment is the eternal damnation of ones immortal soul. And do not think words like immortal and infinity did not scare the living daylights out of me for many years to come. It is one thing to receive a sentence of one kind or another that usually has a definitive time span attached, it is quite another thing to have the sentence go into infinity. I mean what the heck, that is beyond forever – it never stops. Scary stuff. Needless to say, my poor mother was hit with a double whammy. The misery of her grief was augmented by the questions for which she had no acceptable answers.

50. THE HOSPITAL YEARS.

The next three years were the hospital years in which I had some six surgical procedures for one thing or another, mostly trying to correct the inadequacies in the performance of my right leg. Chailey Heritage was an orthopedic hospital/institution for sick children.

Madge, Ron, Mary and Nancy at Chailey

My first encounter there was a truly frightening experience and one that I believe left an indelible mark on my psyche. To start with, the village of Chailey is a long, two bus-ride trip from Cuckfield, taking at least one and half hours if you were lucky with a connection - we still had no family transportation. Mum and Dad took me over there to sign me in, accompanied by my pathetic little travel bag containing my books, my maps, and my mouth organ.

Strange sights of children greeted me in various phases of illness, disabilities, and rehabilitation. Of these, the most frightening and depressing were the victims of the Thalidomide fiasco - women were given this drug for morning sickness and it resulted in hideous birth deformities. Now four or five years later the results had to be dealt with.

My other fellow patients included survivors of the terrible Polio epidemic of the early 1950s, some tuberculosis patients, and one Scottish kid that had been savagely mauled by a leopard through the bars of its cage. These were amazing times. My two best buddies were the aforementioned Jock who had only stumps for arms, and a diminutive boy called Willy Gobels whose growth had been stunted by a severe attack of tuberculosis. He was one of the liveliest and most positive individuals I ever met. We tried to arrange to have our beds side by side so that we could have some fun imagining we were dating one or other of the lovely nurses that passed by our outdoor ward on their way to and from the canteen.

It was a special treat to stay out all night and this privilege was a carrot extended to us patients as a reward for good behaviour, whatever that was interpreted to be. I did not make it very often.

It was really too bad as there was an enormous rookery somewhere close by and each evening at dusk the birds would start their nightly migration to their sleeping perches beginning with ones twos and threes and shortly filling the darkening skies with their wings and sounds. Just to experience this phenomenon was such a welcome break from the long and often miserable days. I actually hated this place. I found it cold, brutal, and staffed with uncaring people who tended a bunch of largely abandoned children.

My parents dropped their visits down to just once a week as it seemed so unfair that I would have lots of visitors while most of my pals had none. Things I saw there left me confused, angry and intolerant of people who do not face their adversities. I saw children running on just their stumps to greet family. I saw what I believed to be physical and mental abuse and maybe worse.

Mum and Dad would make sure they visited with all the children that had no visitors. They would have willingly adopted Willy. He was such a good-natured, happy, non-complaining little boy. One morning I awoke to find his bed empty. I carry him with me to this day.

In Chailey, I became a consummate reader. I read all the classics. I read Shakespeare and Wordsworth. I read history, geography and world affairs. By the time I was finished I was eleven years old, I had missed nearly three years of school off and on, but could hold a half decent conversation with just about anybody on any subject. I could draw a map of the world and every significant country within it. I knew each country's capitol city, largest lake, longest river, and highest mountain. I could draw a map of England including all forty-eight counties. I knew: every British bird and its egg, every airplane, car, wild flower, and tree. I knew every dog. I could identify many of the great composers' works. I knew a Rembrandt from a Renoir. I had a rudimentary understanding of European politics. I was The Renaissance Boy. I know a little about a lot, and a lot about nothing.

In some strange way, I guess I should be grateful to Chailey Heritage. Along with all this, it also reinforced what my parents had instilled in me, and that was never to allow my handicap to be an excuse for not trying something or not giving it my best effort at all times.

51. The Eleven-Plus exams.

In England at this time, there was a system of segregating children into academic and practical course structures at the age of eleven. It was called the Eleven-Plus Exams. Those that passed went to Grammar Schools to become professionals, and those that failed went to Secondary Modern Schools to become tradesmen, truck drivers, or labourers. The exams were in three progressive parts, in other words you had to pass one in order to qualify to take the next. There was no appeal. If you survived the three exams you then had to take an interview to finally gain acceptance for the opportunity for higher education.

Even though I had missed so much school, I whizzed through the three exams and unfathomably failed the interview. I will never for sure know why or how but I suspect the recommendation of the school principal played a large part. I was no one's favourite pupil. I also think that my socio-economic status had an impact. Extra curricular activities at Grammar Schools are subsidized in part by contributions from current students' families and its alumni. Well, they were not going to be getting a hell of a lot from Mr. and Mrs. Knight.

The numbers of available places in Grammar Schools were rather limited, which made it even more competitive to get placed. One thing that became obvious to me was that some of my wealthier, dumber classmates made it to Grammar School while I, and one of my very smart classmates by the name of Sandra, also from Brainsmead, did not.

So all us failures were dumped into Cuckfield County Secondary School. This School opened its doors to students for the very first time in September of 1956. I was one of the first 'First Formers' at the new school. It was quite beautiful. All clean and crisp with bountiful playing fields, carpentry and metalwork shops, science lab and home economics room. It felt good to be there and the quality of staff was of the highest caliber.

Though still managing to get caned now and then, I flourished here. In particular, my English teacher Miss (Joy) Sindon did wonders for me. She channeled my natural propensity to show-off into drama and had me playing lead parts in all her productions. In four successive years, I played The Water Rat in *Toad of Toad Hall*, we did a traditional Chinese play called *Lady Precious Stream*, and we did *Macbeth* and *A Mid-summer's Nights Dream*.

The by-product of all this was that I excelled in English Language, and Literature. Miss Sindon was sister to a popular English actor Donald Sindon who starred in the very successful movie series '*Carry on Doctor*, etc'. She was a sweet, round, confirmed spinster to whom her students were her life. She was also a super exponent of mime. There were times to my discredit that I had the poor woman in tears for which I hope I have made up to her by having a lifetime of pleasure from, and love for, our English language. I have tried at every opportunity to pass this gift along. I wrote to her from Canada many years later to thank her and let her know how I felt.

52. Cuckfield Minors.

The youth club was flourishing. Dad never did accomplish much in the way of extending the club's activities to include boxing, as there just was not the facility for it. He did teach some basic self-defence, for both boys and girls, but mostly it was a general social and sports club. They had some great teams representing the club in Table Tennis, Darts, and all kinds of team sports from athletics to football. The Cuckfield Minors Under Sixteen team, were County champions, as were the Under Eighteens, the latter were quite something.

The Minors needed a home field that would not cost them an arm and a leg to rent so Dad approached a local farmer about using one of his fields. The farmer generously found him a field that was well located just off the main road from Cuckfield to Hayward's Heath. It had character. There were no facilities what so ever, you had to change in the open air – rain, frost, or shine. The field was not exactly flat, there was a long gradual dip on one side that meant a player going down the wing actually all but disappeared from sight for a few strides. The most interesting aspect of the field was that it was home to a veritable colony of moles, so much so, that it became know to all the county as Molehill Stadium.

Dad and I would go out on either Friday evening or first thing Saturday morning to mark the lines on the field using a paintbrush and a bag of lime. The lines were not always that straight and required a bit of fudging imagination on behalf of the linesman during a game, as a player could almost run off the field and back on again without leaving the pitch. The other technicality that had to be overcome on game day was to first usher the cows off the field and then to clear their deposits away prior the first whistle.

Ron Snr, Ron, Geoff Hards, Bob Myers, Bill Boxall, Tony Wells, David Gasson, Tony Bennett, Anthony Hillman, Rodney Paterson, Dave Knape, Stewart Speller.

Great times. I played goal, and made some lifelong friendships as a by-product of this team experience. It was also the birthplace of the Youth Club's own rock band, but more of that later.

One of the neat things about those championship teams is that they were comprised of local boys, either from the village or from the secondary school that drew its students from a little wider area of Mid-Sussex. At one point, I think we had three pairs of brothers, and a threesome of brothers on the team.

Fund-raising for the youth club was a constant in Dad's life. He and Mum would be forever collecting stuff for the next jumble sale, Dad would fix broken things, and Mum would do the washing and mending. I was the promoter and salesman and loved that aspect of it all.

53. Let the Band begin and the Club grow.

While playing on Dad's Minor football team, I met a local lad who attended a private school and then went on to Grammar School in Brighton so I had not actually run into him growing up. Geoff Hards and I shared a love of music and I began meeting with him at his house where he had an empty garage that he used as a recreation room for listening and playing music. He had a guitar, amp, and a mic. I played mouth organ and I had an old child's drum kit. We both sang. We did pop songs of the day from artists like Billy Fury, Cliff Richards, Marty Wilde, and The Everley Brothers. For some time, just the two of us met regularly. I had to get on my bicycle with my drums fitted into one large suitcase balanced on my handlebars and cycle over to Geoff's place, a distance of a mile or so.

Though Dad was the tireless leader of the youth club, Mum gave up a lot for his passion. As well as the fund raising, she had to do without him for two nights a week plus game days, and tournaments of all kinds. She would wash the uniforms after every game as leaving it to each individual player just did not work and Dad hated to see the kids turn up either without their shirts or seeing them caked with mud from the previous game.

The Club would eventually grow out of the church hall and get its own premises down London Lane in which it functioned several nights a week. It was the source of great satisfaction to Dad that he felt that he had to at least in some measure fulfilled his personal commitment to his war buddies. After running the club for seventeen-years he finally accepted a small financial compensation for his work and in truth it came about as a result of him trying to get some pay for the young woman that was helping him. She was a local schoolteacher, a Miss Millband known to us all as Millie, whom I first met when she was terrorized as a student teacher doing a practicum in our class. This was always an open season event and to our shame, we sent many a budding dean of academia screaming into the sunset. Millie survived, and actually returned to become a popular fixture at the school and in the community.

54. PAPER ROUTES, AND MILK RUNS TOO.

From the age of eleven on, I was pretty well financially independent from my parents. They never could afford to give us an allowance and I never would dream of asking them for money. Now I could actually pay my way at home and buy all my own cloths. I had a paper route that started as a five-mile rural trek that I had to do on my bicycle each weekday morning. I picked up my papers down in the village stationers, rode all the way to the bottom of Brook Street and delivered papers all the way back to Whiteman's Green, in all weathers. It took about two hours and I got paid fourteen-shillings a week (less then a dollar). With my first ten-weeks pay I bought myself a brand new metallic-blue Triumph bicycle. It had straight handlebars that were not only sporty but also easier to balance my paper bag on. On Saturdays, I worked with Dad for the local dairy. This involved getting up at 4:30am, and arriving at Gubbin's Dairy to load up the milk-van for the daily route. In the dead of winter, Dad would let me crawl into the furnace room to keep warm while he loaded the van. Man, it was tough to leave that room. I can still see the white-hot glow of the burner and feel its warmth, as I would gently fall asleep.

Being out with Dad was a great time for me. We had so much fun, playing practical jokes on each other, listening to his stories of his youth and war years, or just hanging out. This was my real life education. He taught me the true values that I have tried to hold all my life. A sense of fair play, unbending principles, ethics, compassion, honesty and tolerance - all the contributing aspects to becoming a decent human being. No wonder I have loved him forever, he truly was a great man.

One of the little perks that he would extend to me was that at the end of the route, we would be way out in the country and he would let me drive the van for a short distance. It was a standard transmission so I had to use the clutch and the gears. It was the ultimate in excitement. We would stop in a farm gateway and eat the sandwiches that Mum had prepared for us washed down with a pint of fresh milk. These were truly wonderful days.

Around this time, Uncle Arthur was retiring from window cleaning and sold his motorbike and sidecar to Dad. Wow! This was really something. I loved even the smell of it – the mixture of petrol and leather seemed heaven sent. Just sitting on the bike or kicking it into life was a great thrill. Dad sort of employed me to work with him when I was available, something I would do on and off right up to the time I left England. We had a blast together.

His customers loved him, but I quickly realized that he was grossly undercharging for his services, so I set out to make some adjustments. Within a couple of months I had doubled Dad's income though there were some customers to whom he just could not increase his prices, and I suspect that they paid the same amount right through to Dad's retirement. The neat thing about his additional income from the window cleaning was that he could stop his work at the dairy and just work a normal, if long day.

55. My school days are over.

As the 50s came to a close, so did my school days. I had migrated from my rural paper route to one that went round the wards at Cuckfield Hospital. This was not only a lot more fun but it paid a great deal more as I became a little entrepreneur, selling day, and week-old magazines at half price to patients who would buy anything to break up the boredom of their days. And then there were the nurses. I was quite mature looking for my age and took pride in my appearance resulting in lots of dates with nubile nurses in training. I loved them all – or at least as many as I could get my hands on. The hospital social club would become my favourite hang out for several years. I was earning around two-pounds ten-shillings a week of which I gave ten-shillings to Mum for my keep.

There were many reasons why I decided to leave school at age just sixteen. I had taken and passed all my 'mock GCEs' (General School Certificate), but did not write the actual exams - I kind of lied about this from here on out. Perhaps it was my underlying mistrust of the educational system or simply the fact that even if I managed to get my advanced General School Certificate there was no way that I would ever be able to go to university. My parents just could not afford it. In fact, they needed a better contribution to the household than I was supplying as it was.

Considering all the available trades, it seemed to me that the printing industry offered an avenue of endeavour that would at least border on the artistic, or so I thought anyway. I also had this vague notion even at this time that maybe I could become a 'print buyer' one day. I had read about this function within an advertising agency and it seemed appealing to me. I signed on with a large printing company called Robor Printing Ltd in December of 1960, for the princely sum of three-pounds ten-shillings a week. This allowed me to give Mum a raise of ten-shillings so she got one-pound a week, and I got two-pounds ten-shillings. To give some perspective, a new bicycle would cost fifteen-pounds.

Even at this early stage, I had no tolerance for Trade Unions. In fact, I hated them. For Unions to be so preoccupied with the promotion of mediocrity just went against everything my Dad had taught me about working for a living. Unions - The survival of the least fit? What was that all about? It was Dad's belief that if you accepted a man's pay offering, then you owed him your very best effort at all times and if you could not manage that then you should quit and find another employer.

Being an apprentice also went against the grain, the subservience to the journeyman was more than I could endure. One bloke in particular really got up my nose. Foul mouthed, nasty disposition and disgustingly disrespectful to the female workers in the plant, some of whom of course I had at least my eye on. After a tongue-lashing from him one afternoon, I cornered him in the toilets and let him know that if he ever spoke to me like that again he better defend himself. Of course he ratted on me and I got a warning from above.

The restrictive practices drove me nuts. Never mind the restrictions on what you could do or not do from one trade to another, even as an apprentice there were certain parts of the job that only a journeyman could carry out even if my proximity to the task made eminent sense for me to accomplish it.

Needless to say, my days with Robor were numbered. The day I got my hand caught in the rollers crushing and ultimately losing a finger sort of speeded up my exit. By now I fully understood the mechanics and principals of the offset lithographic process and could competently run a printing press. I had taken all the required courses from camera right through to bindery. This knowledge would serve to carve for me a wonderful career in the future.

I did enjoy having spare money in my pocket and from my first job to my last pay-cheque in England; I bought my Mum flowers on the way home from work every Friday just to see her face. She loved fresh-cut flowers.

56. Rock n' Roll

By now, the whole teenage era was in full swing for me. We went to rhythm clubs in the local towns and villages – rock n' roll was king. The Balcome Hop was the first club that I went to. A hard place to get at: as I had to wait for a bus, then wait for a train, then walk a mile or so, even though it was only about five miles from home. No bar, except pop, but lots of the latest popular tunes played good and loud, and loads of beautiful, eager young girls. Not only my cup runneth over.

I decided to walk home from this club one time. It was a beautiful summer night for a walk. No moon, in fact it was black as the Hole at Calcutta, and not a single vehicle on the road to hitch a ride from. About half the way, home I spotted this motorbike behind a hedge where I had stopped to have a pee. There was not another living sole within two miles. Well I fiddled with it a bit, the bike that is, and low and behold it fired up. Wow! Off I went cheerful as you please. I kept that bike for months, hiding it near home and parking it discreetly at any destination I went to. In the end though, I lost my nerve and gave it up, figuring that it was a matter of time before the Law caught up with me. I dumped it back near where I had 'found' it.

Franklins Village Rhythm Club was a Mecca for kids on Friday nights. It was <u>the</u> place to be. Basically it was just a hall with pop music played loud on a great sound system. Dim lights, no booze, though some would stop by a pub on the way. The girls would come dressed in their finest, and dance together till a pair of lads would split them up. I loved it. In fact, I would split up a pair of girls all by myself and jive with the two of them. This cockiness sometimes attracted some unwelcome attention from either the girls' boyfriends, or just some of the local lads. Either way, I just had to deal with it. Don't get me wrong, I was no hard nut but could answer the bell when called upon.

I was sixteen and getting serious about getting laid. The weather was hot so was the music, and my lovely dance partners all seemed to ware heavy intoxicating perfume. They looked wonderful in their tight-waisted dresses, with multiple crinoline petticoats that swayed to accentuate every beat of the rock tunes. Asking a girl if she would like a lift home was an adventure. She would ask what I had, and I would answer that I had a bike. It was a bit of shock and let down when I got them outside and offered the crossbar of my beautiful blue Triumph bicycle. You have to picture this – several petticoats – crossbar. Yes! Anyway, it all worked out and, as they say, I lost my innocence on a mossy bank out on the common, under a star-studded sky.

Man, we were so naïve. It was all incredibly exiting –and scary too. I do feel sorry for the 'now' generations who it seems see, and hear far to much at a far too young age, which I have to believe takes a lot of the wonderment and mystery out of life's learning.

Two other local hotspots that actually had live bands were up in the 'New Town' of Crawley, at Leon's Club and The Railway Club. The bands, all cover bands in those days, were fantastic. As we did not have much money, we invested our booze allowance in a pint or two of a concoction of cider and Guinness known as 'A Black Velvet'. The theory being that it got you there quickly and economically. These were pretty tough venues, and featured at least one fight every week – some I won, some I did not.

57. Wheels, Wheels, and More Wheels.

Who among us does not remember the day they got their first motor vehicle? With the small amount of compensation I settled for, as a result of losing my finger in the printing press, I bought my first motorbike, a BSA 250 – I was mobile. Never into the heavy leather seen of 'Rocker', and neither prissy nor fashionable enough to be a 'Mod', I sort of hung in a hinterland of my own. I rode a bike but wore suits, cravats, and waistcoats under my all-weather jacket and pants. My white crash helmet had the black horse 'Paladin' on the front, a logo that I still use to this day.

It was great to be able to go either up to Crawley or down to Brighton to a dance and get home under my own steam. It was a lot safer too, as I had been known to jump off the late non-stopping train from Brighton when it slowed down for cross track signals just after Hayward's Heath station. From there I had a short walk across the fields to get home. The live rock bands that played at the Railway Club and Leon's in Crawley really blew me away. I thought they were the cat's meows, and I fantasized being up on stage playing the music.

I did hang out with a great bunch of lads from Hayward's Heath but mostly I ran with the Handcross boys. Among them was Lionel Copeland. He and I were classmates and great pals. And there were several other lads that I met, either in school or playing for the Minors football team. Lionel loved to fight and often dragged me into it so of necessity we became quite efficient. Barry Ray was the senior member of our bunch and did his best to keep us all in line. He had that venerable bearing about him that made him well liked and trusted by all the kids – boys and girls. Barry always made sure that the local girls all got home safely and in one piece from the village dances that were held in various locations around the countryside and beyond. One of our lads, Norman Leopard got the first car in our group. This was a huge deal as it meant we could get to places, and home again warm and dry. His car was a Wolseley, leather upholstery, very posh. And we all had to chip-in for petrol.

The Hayward's Heath Boys. Mike is on the left.

I was the next one to get a set of four wheels, as having split my crash helmet in two after flying through the air; I decided to give my motorbike career a break. I picked up this super old car called Triumph Renown. It looked sort of like a smaller black Rolls Royce but with very angular lines. It smelled of polish and leather and had a huge back seat – a serious plus for a living-at-home young lad in those days.

There was a great nightclub just outside of the town of East Grinstead called The Wiremill Club. It had great bands, roulette, and reasonably priced beer. It was very high class, and the watchful bouncers made sure no riff-raff got in, except us of course. Bill Boxall, Dave Knape, Ronnie Verlander, Barry, and I became regulars.

58. The Pantomime.

One great event that came out of the being involved with the Handcross kids was 'the Pantomime'. I am not too sure who got this thing started. I do know that they persuaded my wonderful English teacher Miss Joy Sindon to Direct. Now to get a bunch of nice average kids, and the inevitable orangutans, to become an acting ensemble is an amazing feat. She did it.

The play was Jack and the Beanstalk. Man, we had a blast doing this. There were times on stage, during a performance, where we just could not control our mirth and had to pause for several minutes to regain a semblance of composure. Every job, on and off stage was performed by one of the kids. We had people holding up falling backdrops when their queue was being called to get on stage. We had curtains unexpectedly rising or falling to reveal the stagehands and actors looking like deer caught in headlights. We had a two-man 'cow' that was about as coordinated as a pregnant camel, and a live chicken that we never did catch so as to appear at the right time to lay the golden egg. The animals never the less stole the show.

I played the Dame Mother Hubbard and got quite comfortable in drag! A newspaper critic summed up the performances thus 'As a theatrical performance it was far from flawless. As an intent to entertain it was priceless.' They were very kind. (I wish they could review this book.)

59. Exit Lionel, enter Mike and Barry.

Lionel had suddenly packed up and gone off to Australia to follow the love of his life and we rarely heard from him ever again. His place as my sidekick was taken over by a lad from Hayward's Heath by the name of Mike Awcock. Mike was the opposite of Lionel. Lionel was a 'Rocker', from the waterfall haircut to the winkle-picker shoes, while Mike was a 'Mod', a gentle, well dressed, quiet spoken lad. I met Mike as a member of a bunch of lads from Hayward's Heath that I went to a Butlin's Holiday Camp with. These dens of iniquity were dotted around the coast of England and though advertised as 'family vacations', were largely patronized by hormone rampant teenagers. We would go to them for a week in a gang of twelve to twenty lads, and we had a ball.

One night we were all barred from entering the main ballroom as we did not have jackets on, and I guess the place did try to maintain some semblance of proprietary. The next night all seventeen of us showed up at the ballroom with jackets white shirts and ties – but no pants. The mêlée that followed resulted in one of our lads being thrown out and the rest of us at least towing some sort of line for the duration.

The next car I got was a 1938 Morris 8. I loved it. It was one of those very boxy looking vehicles sort of like a mini Model T ford. I fixed a Claxon horn onto the side of it and you could hear me coming from miles away. The bodywork was kind of dilapidated and I held it together with thin pieces of sheet metal and self-tapping screws. The engine, all eight horsepower of it was dead easy to work on and I think I took the whole thing to the dump at least twice during its stay with me.

In the summer, Barry and I packed our rucksacks and sleeping bags into my trusty steed and headed for Dover. There we dumped the car behind a hedge and caught the ferry to Ostend, Belgium. From there we hitched-hiked all the way up to Copenhagen. It was a wonderful trip in which we met just super people along the way both fellow travelers and 'rides'. One night we slept on the grass in some bushes on a roundabout just outside of Hamburg. There must have been twenty kids there, few of whom could speak each other's language. It was amazing how well we got along, leaving each other early the next morning with hugs of farewell. Denmark is notably clean and fresh looking, from its countryside, and streets to its people. I enjoyed this trip no end, even though I froze my nuts off most nights. I mentioned earlier that I packed my sleeping bag. Well, in truth it was a relic from my short-lived Boy Scout days comprised of two blankets and a bunch of safety pins.

This was a real bonding trip for Barry and I that would endure forever, and pave the way for some great visits in our futures for he, and his lovely wife Josie, whom he met one night at a dance in Reigate that he and I went to.

Dad was also now four-wheeled. I got him into a neat Austin van, fitted with a back seat. Mike's dad, who was a panel-beater by trade and did up old cars as a sideline, had rebuilt it. Mum and Dad were quite chuffed they could now get out and about a bit at leisure and in comfort, plus Dad had a work vehicle that would take his ladders, and somewhere warm and dry to eat his lunch. It was sad to say goodbye to his motorbike and sidecar and I do recall taking it for one last two-wheel blast up Cuckfield High Street.

60. The Deputies.

One day, quite out of the blue I got a call from one of the village lads, a Tony Wells. I had played on the football team with Tony but as he was a couple of years older than me, had not had much to do with him otherwise. He, along with Geoff Hards, who was now married with a daughter, were going to form a rock band and wanted to know if I was interested in playing drums. The forth member of the band was going to be another Cuckfield lad by the name of Roger Heath.

Tony Wells, Ron, Geoff Hards, Roger Heath.

Our first meeting was in a field near Tony's house. The four of us: Roger on lead, Geoff on rhythm and lead vocal, Tony on bass, and me on drums. It was all rather primitive as only Tony had ever actually played in any kind of band, and that was trumpet in a brass band. And though Geoff could play a few chords, no one was very competent with either guitars or drums.

We started practicing at least three or four nights a week either in Tony's front room or at Geoff's house. How either family put up with it heaven knows – we were noisy. We also were starting to be quite good. A name had to be decided on and as Tony, our bandleader's nickname was Marshal, we settled on 'the Deputies'.

New year's eve 1961, we played our first gig in the cricket club hall at the tiny village of Ansty. Our repertoire lasted maybe an hour and for the rest of the night we did 'requests'. It went very well considering, and all seemed to have a great time. It did not take very long after this that we learned enough tunes to be able to play for several hours without repeating.

It was the early 60s. A time of the Cold War, when fear of the Russian evil empire, launched a lanky, virtually unknown Scottish actor, into instant stardom as 007. A time when an upstart fashion designer named Mary Quant from a tiny shop in Soho invented the miniskirt and with the help of a skeletal waif by the name of Twiggy rocked the established 'rag trade'. And speaking of rock, four mop-headed, Mod lads from Liverpool along with four rebellious students from the London School of Economics hijacked and Anglicized American rhythm & blues music, and fostered the British Invasion of the pop music world.

Ron, Tony, Geoff, Roger, Nigel.

Playing in the band to a large extent was my salvation as it gave me somewhere to channel my energy, creativity, and spare time, and it endowed me with a good deal of responsibility that kept me off the proverbial street corners.

We quickly upgraded our song list and thanks to Dad's efforts through the youth club, we also upgraded our instruments. We started to look good and sound great. My functions with the band included that of Booking Manager and Driver. I was the only band member with a driving license. I had upgraded to a Mini and yes, there is such a thing as love in a Mini as long as it did not need to share the space with my drum kit!

We were very frugal with our earnings and bought a Thames passenger van that held all our burgeoning equipment, the four of us and a 'techy'. I got the band gigs throughout southern England. All the village halls that we had frequented as revelers were now our venues including the ever so swish Wiremill Club.

To fill out the sound we had added a tenor sax, originally played by our pal Norman but he also had commitments to another dance band called the Consorts so he was replaced with Nigel. The sax really did typical 'Buddy Holly' and 'Shadows' line up of Lead, Rhythm, and Bass, plus Drums. Our line-up also changed. Roger left, Tony moved to Lead, and another Roger (Hensley), came on board at Bass.

61. A TASTE OF THE 'BIG TIME'.

A friend of Dad's, George Stevenson sort of fancied himself as an impresario as was his brother. I think George (Mr. Steve), who was a grocer by trade, rather envied his brother's lifestyle and saw The Deputies as his ticket to the big-time. He was a thoroughly decent person and did indeed get us some great work. He became our manager though I continued to book all the local stuff – our bread and butter. Unfortunately, Mr. Steve was also a dreamer and I am afraid that all our earnings went to promoting the band and for fancy clothes for us to ware. Never the less we played with the very best, and top bands of the day - The Hollies, The Bachelors, The Mindbenders, Them (Van Morrison), The Searchers and my forever favourite, Dusty Springfield. She had just left her original folk/country trio 'The Springfields' to take on a pop solo career when we played with her at a concert on the Isle of Wight. She was lovely and easy to talk to. We shared a soda together.

We played at wonderful theatres all over England culminated by doing the famed 'Sunday Night at the London Palladium'. This was 'The Show' in England at that time, with a huge TV audience.

We also did a tour of Germany as part of a Variety Show, which played at NATO bases from Munich to Hamburg. This tour gave me my first airplane ride. We travelled on the famous Comet that was the first ever jet airliner – what a thrill. I think the impressions of my fingers are likely still on those armrests.

Our biggest and best fans were from the Cuckfield Youth Club. Dad and Millie would organize coach loads of screaming kids to attend our concerts. We really did feel like pop stars though all of us had regular jobs, and indeed, this was hard to juggle at times.

One night we were sharing the billing with a popular 'Trad Jazz' band by the name of Kenny Ball at the Corn Exchange, which was part of the Regency-styled Dome in Brighton. After the interval, Kenny and his band were on the stage and I happened to be still at my drums fiddling around. Kenny's drummer must have been in the 'loo' or something. Anyway he called out 'everybody ready: One - two, one, two, three, four', and there we were right into *Alexander's Ragtime band.* A great thrill.

Unfortunately, we never quite got over that hump that would make the band-work life-style sustaining. Our popularity remained very localized in the south of England where our records did ok but we never could breakout onto the national or international stage. We were a good, clean-cut cover band with a wide appeal in terms of age groups. We did big ballads and Rock 'n' Roll.

I also did some free-lance drumming on the side, and got to play with some good bands. I was no great drummer, but looked good, could sing, and keep time. My business card had the black Paladin on it and read 'Have Drums Will Travel' a take off of a popular TV western series. I have used this logo in one form or another ever since.

62. Sheila Weds.

Sister Sheila was always the rebel, and she and Mum were doomed never to see eye to eye. (Ironically, it would be Sheila that was Mum's champion at her life's end.) When Sheila was ready for high school, there were just two Catholic school options – Crawley or Uckfield, both at least a forty-five minutes to a one-hour bus ride away. It was decided that she would go to Crawley.

Crawley was one of several massive urban developments that sprang up in the '50s, with the intent of relieving the pressure off London. They were referred to as 'New Towns'. These were a collection of neighbourhoods that were complete with schools, shopping centres, and entertainment.

Mum, Ellen, Fred, Christine, Sheila, Dad, Ron, Mrs. Wakeham.

Populated for the most part by displaced Londoners these towns brought their share of city problems to the Sussex countryside. Sheila embraced this lifestyle and left school as soon as it was legal, to take an apprenticeship in ladies hairdressing. She was a good-looking young woman who got more then her fair share of attention from the jet-set males in the area. She however, just to be au contraire, took up with the father of one of her fellow apprentices. Entre Fred Wakeham. Fred was the same age as Dad so you can imagine how that went over at home. He was also a divorcee – oh boy, that's not good. Fred was indeed a much older man but he was also quite modern in a nice way. He did not wear young men's clothes or try to look younger than he was but he dressed very conservatively well. He had a good job and by our standards certainly, was well off. His only concession to youth was perhaps his MG sports car.

I liked him a lot, and I must admit I was quite prepared not to. His passion was Dixieland Jazz, which I also came to really appreciate and enjoy.

So, when Sheila turned twenty-one, the age of consent, much to Mum's consternation she married Fred. They had many fine years together producing three great offspring – Liza, Dan, and Ben.

Unfortunately the age thing would catch up with them eventually ending in a non-acrimonious divorce.

63. Frustrated with the English system.

Working as a printer was just not fulfilling enough for me. It paid very well but I was bored. Once the press was set up to run, the challenge was over and I would just sit by the side of it and read a novel. I bounced around a few work places and the most interesting was a small place in Burgess Hill that was a photographic firm that also did some colour printing. I got the job as the pressman but was also exposed to (no pun intended) the art of photography -that really peaked my interest. I started to go out on assignments when the press was idle, and loved it. Sadly, the firm, which was the pastime of a rich man's wife, went under, and we were all out of work.

Dad got me an interview with a customer of his who owned a business equipment company up in Reigate, Surrey. I got the job as sales representative and neatly dressed, with my brand new, Wedgewood-blue and gunmetal-gray Triumph Herald to show off in, started my training. This likely could have worked out very well for me but there were a couple of elements that were becoming ever more pervasive in my life – the travel bug and the British class system.

On careful reflection I have concluded that it was not the class system in of itself that bothered me, it was the fact that the upper echelons would never have let me join. I am in fact for my sins, an elitist, which is a bit of an anachronism, in that it was this system, employed by the educational establishment, which had robbed me of my chance at higher learning. I actually like the class system with a few at the top supported by a broad base at the bottom – like a pyramid. Everyone, or at least most, knew their place and were largely accepting of it. A pyramid is after all a very stable piece of geometry providing it stays on its broad base. If too many climb to the top, it inverts and topples over. The problem today is that we no longer have a pyramid in the western democracies we have an egg. The masses have been allowed to abandon the base and aim for the top, and though never able to attain it they, and we, are stuck with this massive girth called the middle classes.

Though I was working hard at this time I was not really getting ahead, I had only enough savings in my bedroom drawer to go on a modest vacation once a year. The two weeks off seemed grossly inadequate. There was, in my mind anyway, a major holdback to me getting ahead inherent in the British class system, not to mention my fundamental lack of formal education. All this culminated in my looking into emigration. I checked out Australia, New Zealand, and Canada.

In the early 60s, England was a Mecca for 'au pair girls'. These were teenage girls from the mainland of Europe who were sort of employed by English families as nannies. They got room and board and a little money in exchange for their work. One reason for them being in-service was to travel a little but mostly it was to perfect their English. As far as I was concerned, they were put solely on this planet to beautify my environment. I just loved their exotic looks and accents and their liberal attitudes towards male female relationships. Of the Europeans, the Scandinavians were the most gorgeous.

They were all wonderful but one in particular blew me away. Torunn was the penultimate Viking Princess – long-limbed, blond, and blue-eyed. She came from way up the Norwegian coast in the land of the midnight sun. We had a wonderful year together and actually attended sister Ellen and Roy's wedding as a couple just prior to them leaving for Canada. This romance I had taken seriously for the first time in my life but it ended quite suddenly – I was dumped in favour of a return to her home in Norway. Women are much more practical then men about such things. She realized that she could never permanently reside anywhere but among the lakes and fjords of her native land - and that I could not.

64. FAREWELL TO THE 'LAND OF MY FATHERS'.

There was a particular allure about Canada that I derived from watching movies, showing trains roaring through the Rockies, guarded by the red serge jacketed Mounties. These and the fact that my younger sister Ellen had moved to Vancouver Island prompted me to make a date with Canada House.

There were stringent rules and requirements regarding the qualification of emigrants to Canada. It went on some kind of point system, and you were awarded for things like health, age, education, work experience, and what your job ambitions were in relation to your preferred location destination. Having heard a lot of flattering things about Vancouver, it was my first choice and I put down both printing and sales as my employment objective. My medical went well and it was the first and likely only time I was ever listed as being 'a fraction under six feet' (5ft 11-3/4"), a description I have been quite content to carry since. The total result for me was that I was cleared to immigrate to New Westminster in 'Sales'. Don't ask me, I have no idea why that town, about twenty-miles away, would have more sales openings than Vancouver.

I just made it to Ellen and Roy's wedding before finalizing my departure date.

From this point on things moved very quickly and I had a flight booked for two months hence. Now came the bustle of selling my car that at this time was a black and white Austin Metropolitan that I bought cheap after I turned in my lovely, dented Triumph Herald that had met the bank of a country lane one fine frosty night. Next went my drums, which I got far to little for in the Brighton Lanes. My fortune now was up to three hundred and seventy five Pounds. I packed the rest of my entire life into one large suitcase that I would live out of, off and on for the next seven years. The cost to me for my one-way trip was three hundred and fifty dollars but this was paid for me by the Canadian Government against a promissory note to pay it back in installments as soon as I gained full employment.

One of what would be many such sad days was the day I said goodbye to my Mum and Dad. Dad was quite stoic in the true stiff upper lip tradition. We had had many opportunities for conversation leading up to this move, as I had worked with him for a couple of months prior to leaving. Not surprisingly, I had his total support. Poor Mum could not rationalize the loss of a second child and her only son to far away Canada. As far as she was concerned, Columbus, Hudson and Eric the Red should all have stayed at home. She was desperate and no amount of consoling was much help. It was just not fair and looking back on it, she was right. No matter how many times over the next forty-years (and there would be lots) that I left her it would be a heart rending experience. She deserved better. Thank goodness Ellen did not settle in Canada and after a couple of years, she, Roy and their two daughters went back home.

For me it was just an adventure, another chapter in my life. I had adopted some basic philosophy when in hospital those years ago that said never regret anything, face every move in life as a living reality, and deal with it. Regrets just lead to self-pity. Never hunger after that which you do not have, unless you are prepared to work towards it. Avoid comparison - it is the ultimate depressant as there will always be someone better off. Always look forward. If you come to a fork in the road, take one.

October 19, 1966. It was a Wednesday when I boarded the Stretch DC 8 at Heathrow airport my mind full of a mass of different emotions. As the plane lifted off and soared into the clouds, I remember saying goodbye to Sussex not knowing when I would see it again – if ever. Canada was a long way away in those days. What lay ahead was a mystery. It was not that there was a master plan; it was just a case of let's see what happens next.

One thing for sure was that I was on my own. There was no financial safety net either out there or back home. I would sink or swim according to my own financial schedule, and the same goes for my emotional wellbeing. Some of the things that went through my mind were a litany of the events that had brought me to this point and these culminated in the belief that I could be, and do, better then I had managed so far. The new land was an opportunity to be anything I said I was as there was only me to contradict it. I could say anything I liked and as long as I lived up to any expectation that I extended things would work out just fine.

65. OH CANADA.

The plane touched down in the prairie province of Saskatchewan at Saskatoon to unload some passengers and re-fuel. We de-planed while they gassed up. Descending down to the tarmac and walking through the cold dark October morning to the terminal building, I bent down and touched the ground as a gesture of arrival.

The plane flew us on to Vancouver arriving to clear sunny skies, obviously a good omen. Meeting the plane was sister Ellen, Roy, and their new baby Michelle. First stop was our Aunt Daphne's place where we were going to stay the night before going over to Vancouver Island, a two-hour ferry-ride from Vancouver across the Straits of Georgia.

Daph's husband, Uncle Bill, was an interesting man to talk to. He had charm, was very quiet spoken and always interested in hearing other points of view. His hobby was rock hounding. That entailed scrambling over the banks and bars of rivers searching for precious, and semiprecious stones, and gold. His collection was kept in large glass cases that looked like and in fact likely were fish tanks. They were either brightly lit or 'black lit' to show off their contents among which were faceted replicas that he had made, of all the worlds' most famous gems. We also met our 'Moldowin' cousins – Terry, Manny, Daphne, Evelyn, and Melody – quite a house full.

The next morning we were up, breakfasted, and off on the one-hour drive to the ferry and what a spectacular drive it was. From the town of Richmond where Aunty Daph lived, close to the airport, the view of the Coast Mountains is the most panoramic of any vista of them available anywhere. From there, we drove north, right through downtown Vancouver, across the famed Lionsgate Bridge, up and along the new Upper Levels Highway, before descending into the picturesque Horseshoe Bay ferry terminal. The weather for late October was spectacular and the sights around me seemed to fulfill all my imaginings of what Canada should look like. The two-hour ferry ride across the Straits of Georgia to Nanaimo and the one and a half hour drive to Port Alberni was just icing on the cake.

And then it rained. And it rained. I was seriously considering drawing up plans for an Arc. I'm not kidding. The next forty days and forty nights it rained without letup, while I was pounding pavement trying to find work, any work. My first job was tree planting – I nearly died. Planting trees on a near vertical slope, in November, in the peeing rain, has to be experienced to appreciate. Our crew boss was a behemoth of man. I kept looking around for a blue ox! First he gave me the gear. A hard-hat, rain gear, a pick, and cork boots – though why they call them cork beats me. Isn't cork supposed to be light? Then he strapped a pouch containing a few dozen tree-saplings to my waist. I looked like a refugee from The Village People. Next came the work demonstration. 'Arnie' in a simple series of effortless motions, took one giant step forward, swung his pick at the permafrost and produced a divot into which he placed a sapling from his pouch. His next stride firmed the plant in place and he moved on. No problem. Right? No! I am on a forty-five degree slope on the side of a mountain. It is pissing with rain. I take a huge swing with my pick and as it strikes the ground I am reminded of one of those old cartoons in which the vibrations move back up the handle causing the holder to do an impression of a jackhammer. Oh man, and I thought I was tough - I lasted one day.

Finally, I managed to get a job working for a large department store called Woodward's as a sales clerk in the hardware department, after having to shave off my beard as a concession to their clean-shaven hiring policy. This should have been a warning of things to come but at the time, income – any income, was the all-encompassing motivation. With my first pay-cheque I bought an old car, a 1953 Ford, an enormous beast with lots of bright chrome, powered by a pounding V8 engine. Once again, I was elated with the joy of being mobile.

I actually owe a lot to the town of Port Alberni as in my short stay there I learned to play Bridge properly, and I played my first guitar chords, to the tune of House of the Raising Sun, both these endeavours are primary in my life today.

My career in the 'Port' ended quite dramatically when while posted to the gas station pumping gas I managed to get into an altercation with a huge logger over being whistled at to get attention. I turned the water hose into his cabin, nearly broke his leg slamming the car door back at him as he tried to get to me. What else could I do, if he had caught me he would have killed me. Oh well, not the first time I had been fired and it would certainly not, by any means, be the last.

66. Launched from Third Beach.

With my now famous suitcase and guitar packed into the trunk of the Ford, off I went to Vancouver where I lived in its opulent back seat on Third Beach in English Bay, thanking goodness for a warm, very early spring.

The kids I met on the beach shared whatever they had and I reciprocated as best I could, though to begin with that was very little. I was running out of cash for gas, so the Ford had to be parked in favour of bread. Each day I would walk to one of the big hotels and into its washroom, there to shave and dress for job hunting – yes, I kept the beard off, as I just could not afford the possibility of any additional prejudice. I was hungry, lonely and broke. It could only get better.

It was spring of '67 and flower power was nearing its zenith accompanied by its 'peace brother' and free love. I got a little job working for a chemical plant in Richmond printing their labels. It was steady income and afforded me the luxury of renting a bed-sitter on 25th Avenue at Main. It was from there that I dropped into a small printing company on Main Street called Modern Printers and was offered an immediate job as Pressman and General Manager.

Hey! I had arrived. Now that's more like it. This person was going to make me a partner; it was everything I had imagined for myself. I could write home and tell the folks that the boy had made good. Oh well, so much for that perception. Ultimately the only claim to fame I achieved here was to print the 2nd and 3rd editions of a radical newspaper called The Georgia Straight. This was a gas. We would write the classifieds ourselves in order to attract readership and more advertising. We would say things like 'Horny chick looking for dumb stud to share apartment'. It worked. This ragtag hippy newspaper would survive the test of time to become mainstream in the '90s.

In spite of this modest success, I was all but overcome by of all things, the loneliness. Coming from a big extended family in England I was used to a constant coming and going of people that I knew well. To find myself in a one-room lodging with practically no money and no company was hard. One Friday night I went downtown and happened to drop into a very lively looking beer-parlour called The Devonshire. It was packed. So much so that there were no free tables, and in Canada you were not allowed to stand up and drink which resulted in me squishing onto the end of a large semi-circular booth. My companion to my left was also alone. He kind of stuck out in that he had quite a suntan for April. Conversation with Gerry soon reviled that he was a skier and had managed to get early sunburn on the slopes of Whistler Mountain and Mount Baker.

This night was the turning point for me. I think without it I might just have packed up and gone home defeated with my tail between my legs. Gerry was on his way to a party and asked me why not come along to 'Australia House'. It was a wild bash and effectively conjured up an instant social life from which I never had to look back.

I joined the YMCA Ski Club as a social member, which meant I was a beer drinker, not a skier – I could not yet afford the latter. We all met at a pub every Thursday night where we threw a dollar in the pot which would produce five small glasses of beer and given the fact that many of the girls drank very little one could get a pretty good buzz on for two bucks. The club also ran excursions to Mount Baker in Washington State, and more regular trips to Whistler Mountain, where we stayed in some tiny 'A' frames at Brandywine Falls, packed to the rafters head to toe like sardines. It was my kind of place. It was so crowded that I swear to God I got laid twice just trying to get to the washroom and back.

The road to Whistler was something else. A twisting two-lane highway went north out of Vancouver and hugged the coast all the way up to the town of Squamish. Correct that, it hugged the side of the fjord and at times seemed to hang out over the Howe Sound. There was a constant threat of landslides that claimed the lives of travelers each and every year. The next 100km up into the mountains was on either dirt, or graded gravel roads. It was a tough choice as to which was worse, the rock slides or the possibility of skidding over a cliff that could take you down a couple of thousand feet into the Cheakamus Canyon.

I did eventually become a competent après-skier. I could talk the talk when called upon plus I could play some folk songs, and a selection of old Rock n' Roll on an old Framus guitar that I had picked up in Port Alberni.

67. THE RANCH AND THE GREAT DANE.

One morning at Modern Printers, in walked a strikingly good-looking young couple. He was blonde, blue eyed with broad shoulders and an easy laugh. She was taller then he with reddish hue to her very light brown hair. Leo was a hand compositor, which is a typesetter using moveable type from trays to build pages of print. He was hired, and he and Eva would become my closest friends for years to come. They were Danish and for some reason, likely Mum's background, I have long held an automatic affinity with people from Scandinavia. They just seem to have that fresh, clean, honest look about them. Leo liked to laugh, party, drink beer, and fight on occasion. He was my kind of guy, and game for anything, at any time, anywhere.

The Ranch is a book all by itself and maybe someday I will just have to get down to writing it, but one thing at a time.

One of the twice a year excursions that the ski club organized was a long weekend at a guest ranch in the Cariboo. The Cariboo is in the central interior of British Columbia. It is ranch land, cowboy country. Massive expanses of open grasslands dotted with soda-pot lakes and stands of Jack Pine.

To get there was a four to five-hour drive depending on how you valued your life. The road took you East up the fertile valley of the mighty Fraser River to the junction at the town of Hope where the road north follows the old gold-rush wagon track through the Fraser Canyon. Once again a perilous trek to be sure, with lots of hairpin bends and a constant need to be on the lookout for potential avalanches attested to by the regular and sudden appearances of boulders of all sizes in the middle of the road. These hints of danger just made the prospect of the trip that more exciting and Leo, Eva, and I signed up in a flash for the Easter Weekend. The cost was really cheap when I think back on it, and especially if compared to today's vacations. The main reason for the price break was that it was pre-season, as the guest ranches did precious little business prior to June 1st each year due to the climate. This weekend was their opportunity to have a ranch full of people, top off their horses, and test their organization. The ski club packed up to sixty people into the resort.

The big day came. It was Friday straight after work when our car pool comprised of the three of us and three other club members set off in Leo's 1958 Chevrolet Impala station-wagon full of excitement and anticipation for the weekend to come. Common sense, yes we did have a little, kept us from having any beer during the drive up. That is until we reached the end of the paved road at Cache Creek where we pulled over for a wee-wee break and cranked open our first beer. The star filled sky was alight. Never had I seen such an array. The Milky Way was a vast swath of stars crossing the heavens above us.

The last eleven miles was on a graded dirt and gravel road whose turn to be graded had long come and gone. The result was like driving on a washboard. The beer helped even if it frothed a little both in the 'stubby' bottle and in the gullet. We had been given good instructions and directions how to get into Beaverdam Guest Ranch including the need to go exactly eleven miles on this track and look for the small sign indicating Beaverdam Lake. There it was and three minutes later, we were back in the late 1800s.

The guest ranch was comprised of one main street – dirt of course, with small one-room log cabins on either side, about fourteen in all, plus the main ranch house and the cookhouse, all this by the side of a beautiful, pristine lake. It was here that I heard for the first time the true call of the Canadian wild – The Loon. This haunting, melancholy sound still gives me goose bumps whenever I hear it and makes me long for those days of yore.

An old cowboy by the name of Orville Federspiel greeted us – no, I did not make that name up. He was tall; lean, bandy legged, with lots of white hair, and owned the ranch that he ran with his wife, son, and daughter-in-law. After signing in and being assigned a cabin to drop off our gear, we headed down to the cookhouse that doubled as the lounge - and the party was on.

Next morning we were up with the cockerel, we had little choice actually, noisy buggers, and after a full breakfast of bacon, sausages, and pancakes, we trundled off to the main coral to meet our trusty steeds. The horse-wranglers were a breed unto themselves, and I must say in all the years that I would play and work with cowboys and horsemen I met few that I did not like. My first two were bloody marvelous. Cactus was in fact a boy from Malta that had come to Canada as a young lad and embraced the horse culture in a big way. He would never leave. A great storyteller and I do mean stories. We quickly learned that you had to take anything he said with a bucket of salt. He was a charmer and had all the young kitchen staff, and housemaids, and guests, eating out of the palm of his hand.

The other guy was a swarthy dark-skinned good-looking man with a droopy moustache and piercing eyes that if plugged into a grid could have lit Vancouver. He passed himself off as a Mexican but we soon discovered that he was in fact second or even third generation Canadian East Indian. Tab Shori was the greatest. Not only did he know all there was to know about horses, he loved to pass on that knowledge in a way that made instant converts to the cowboy-way out of a very diverse assembly of 'dudes'.

I drank it all in like a man dying of thirst. Tab was also a fine guitar player-singer and we would jam together for years to come. He kind of took a liking to me. I wore a flat topped, black cowboy hat and a pauncho. The combination seemed to remind him of the Spaghetti Westerns and my natural vanity encouraged this association. One of my favourite Tab songs was his rendition of 'Everybody's Talking at me' from the film *Midnight Cowboy*. I still think of Tab whenever I hear that song. Tab was the consummate cowboy who wandered around the Cariboo mostly working the guest ranch circuit. I visited with him many years later and proudly introduced him to my boys. Such a fine man in so many ways, unfortunately, Tab failed to fend off his own demons and I fear drank himself to death – a terrible waste of a fine human being.

We were all assigned a horse for the weekend according to our riding experience and of course, Leo and I were both 'experts' so we got the most rang-a-tang nags in the whole remuda. Baptism by fire I guess you would call it but we learned. Fast. The rides took us way out into the wilds of the range country for the whole morning ending up on the bank of one of a series of lakes that were linked like a string of sausages. They called them the Chain Lakes, and it was there that the chuck wagon and staff met us with hamburgers, hotdogs, and all the fixings, for a lunch to soothe the kind of hunger that the great outdoors seems to incubate. They would also throw in a couple of beers to soothe the savage saddle sores.

By the time we got back to the ranch, dismounted, and put our tack away we could hardly stand but it was happy hour so no peace for the wicked. A few tinnies, a huge meal, and the jukebox would be thumping out Rock n' Roll. The party was back on and continued way into the wee hours. It seemed that we had no sooner let our heads hit the pillow when it was breakfast call and guess what - we did it all again.

68. Enter Ethel. Go East young man.

Back in Vancouver on the way to a party one Friday evening, I was picking up some beer at the liquor store on Howe Street after work, and got in the line-up with a couple of girls who seemed to have lots to say for themselves. I ended up getting the phone number of the particularly yappy blonde. The following week I drummed up the courage to dial the number and made a date with Ethel Swedahl. Again, my weakness for the Scandinavian came to the fore.

She was the daughter of a Norwegian couple that lived and worked out of a fishing community along the Fraser River in Surrey. She was a schoolteacher in the Surrey school district and lived in a rented apartment in New Westminster. We started seeing each other regularly but not exclusively as she was planning to move back east for the summer after the school year ended June 30th.

Timing is everything – right? Our boss at the print shop turned out to be a real crook. What he did on a regular base was to hire dumb emigrants like us, fill them with hopes, and then after a while simply stop paying them. Oh, he would string it out for as long as he could with the story that he was owed a big cheque and if we could just hold on a little longer he would be able to pay us up and make it worth our while. We finally figured it out that he had no intention of paying us, and I could not string along anyway. I had no money. On top of this I got rear-ended, my car written off, and though it was no fault of mine, not only could I not claim due to the fact that I did not have insurance but I had to surrender my license until such time as the perpetrator of the collision signed off – which they were in no hurry to do. Ethel had left for Toronto. A friend of mine from the ski club was also planning to try his employment luck back east and was leaving in his VW Bug on the weekend. I packed my suitcase and guitar and we drove the four thousand miles east – have guitar will travel.

We did the drive across western Canada with three stops: Banff, Winnipeg, and Kenora 'Lake of the Woods'. It was great to be out on the open road and just going. A pleasure I will always find alluring. Banff and Kenora were lovely towns and stand out in my mind more than much in between. Tony and I arrived in Toronto in the middle of a heat wave and after hooking up with Ethel found cheap digs at a Campus Co-op on Spedina Avenue right near the University. It suited our needs very well and I managed to get a job quite near there at a small printing plant, running a couple of presses – yes you read it right, they expected me to operate two presses at one time. One for quick runs while the other was doing a long run. This might have been doable except that I had not operated a press in the past couple of years, and my make-ready was a little rusty therefore rather slow. I got fired – again, but not before I had gained a few weeks experience so that when I went to my next job, which happened quite quickly, I could handle the workload without any trouble.

The summer of '67 was a good time for me. It was hotter then hell. Toronto is a big cosmopolitan city with lots of first-line entertainment including some of the best jazz clubs in North America. We went to see Gene Krupa, The Modern Jazz Quartet and lots of other big name entertainers. 1967 was also the year of the world's fair in Montreal, Expo'67. We drove up there for a weekend and I loved Montreal for its flair, food, and European pizzas. As sure as the summers are hot, the winters are not, and there does not seem to be any noticeable segue between the two. It was quite a new experience to walk out of a building and drop one hundred degrees in temperature.

Ethel was heading back to Vancouver so I decided to go home for Christmas on a cheap flight that turned out to be the slow plane to London. It was likely one of the last flights of the four engine turboprops, the Loughheed Constellation. We flew from Toronto to New York to London a journey of some twenty-hours.

It was super to see all the family and friends again but even though I had only been away for less then two years, things had moved on without me with no trouble at all. I actually felt a bit of a stranger in my own land, more so on this first of dozens of trips then on any that would follow. On future visits my expectations would be more realistic, and I would recognize the fact that I was indeed the stranger and intruder, and conduct myself accordingly. I did land a great job while there however, starting as a press-operator at the local newspaper, The Mid-Sussex Times and ending up in sales, selling advertising space. It is quite possible that this would have been an interesting and successful career path for me but I missed Ethel and I still felt that I had short-changed myself in the new land. I decided to give Vancouver one more serious attempt to make a place for myself in the world. I bought another one-way ticket back to Vancouver, said even more painful goodbyes to Mum and Dad and took once again to the skies.

69. Fidelity Life Assurance Company.

Ethel met me at the airport and I moved into her apartment in New Westminster. I found myself back on the streets, pounding it out looking for work. One thread led to another and perhaps the luckiest meeting of my young life work-wise, was with a man by the name of Jim Alexander at The British Columbia Institute of Technology. Jim was an instructor, a master typographer, and loved to chat. I guess he liked me, I know I respected him, and as it turned out we would be fierce, but great competitors in our futures. He told me that he had heard that there was a position open with an insurance company running their in-house printing department.

I scooted right over there and was hired on the spot. This was a real break for me. The print shop serviced a pair of associated companies, Fidelity Life and Century Insurance.

We designed, typeset, assembled, and printed all their insurance forms and promotional publications. I had two employees running the presses while I ran the operation. I came up with ideas for sales incentives, and I was the purchasing agent for any item or printed piece that we did not have the equipment to produce ourselves. I also did the inventory, bookkeeping; made sure the shelves were stocked, and assured the correct application of government taxes. I learned on the job.

Ethel and I decide to be married, and after being turned down by the Catholic Dioceses of Vancouver over a dispute as to the upbringing of any children from the marriage, we had our ceremony performed by a kind of a renegade priest named Fr. Roberts of Port Moody. We had no money and nor did her mother so the event was quite modest, and following it we took off for a trip in my TR3 Triumph sports car, all the way down to Tijuana Mexico.

The job was going very well so much so that I found myself with extra capacity in the print shop, which got my imagination going on what to do with that spare press-time. I came up with a carefully documented business plan by where I would solicit work from within and around our building. The profits would be shared between the Company and yours truly. While my boss was keeping my proposal under advisement, another far-reaching set of circumstances was in spin.

The banking system in Canada was and still is very well regulated and as part of this, insurance companies were, among other things, not allowed to sell securities. However this suddenly changed to the degree that they were now allowed to initiate their own Mutual Fund and sell shares to their subscribers. This was a big new deal, and I was charged with the design and production of the inaugural prospectus for The Century Growth Fund. Well, as one of my heroes would say 'A man has to know his limitations' and I knew that the design of this piece was too important to be thrown together by myself. I went to the yellow pages and under graphic design firms; I saw a company called Ad Art Associates. I picked up the phone and dialed.

This started a series of events that would govern my working life and my career for the next twenty years. The graphic designer that came to see me was an impressive German fellow. He was tall, good-looking, confidant, and exuded old-world charm. Jurgen Grohne and I became business associates. I would use his talents whenever a serious design assignment came up.

One evening I got a call from Jurgen telling me that his younger brother Frithjof was immigrating to Vancouver and had secured a job similar to mine at the West Coast Transmission Company. The only caveat was that he was going to be expected to run a press the like of which he had never seen before. Frithjof was a printer but used to operating huge presses not these little machines that we used in an in-plant situation. Jurgen asked if I would mind giving 'Joff' a crash course. This was not a problem and Joff and I met in our print shop and would become friends for life.

70. My marriage ends.

Work was going well. Ethel and I were not. To this day, I would not be able to identify any real build up of discontent, certainly not on my part. We had our differences of opinion on lots of subjects that is true. Politics: she was as hard left as I was right. She was always looking for a cause or perhaps they found her. She would actively protest important issues like the Vietnam War when most people though that Dien Bien Phu was a tropical disease. She was a contemporary of, not a follower of Gloria Steinem, and an ardent supporter of human and female rights. She suffered fools poorly on either of these subjects. She was protesting whale and baby seal hunts several years before the foundation of Green Peace. We argued about these things but not bitterly. I am aware on reflection that I was stupidly jealous of anyone she gave attention to. I was incredibly possessive to the point of suffocation perhaps. As a naturally outgoing person who loved socializing and debating, I can see that this was difficult for her. There were also the home lifestyle issues. Not that I was exactly a 'Susie Homemaker' but I did have a problem with the place being a mess at all times, and no doubt considered this more her responsibility then it was mine. I came home for lunch one day to find she and her mother moving her out. Not that we had much to begin with and most of it I suppose was hers having had it given to us from her family as wedding presents. I grabbed the electric frying pan and planted myself on the bed so they could not take that. They did leave me a knife, fork and spoon.

I was broken-hearted. Devastated in fact. Marriage was very important to me and I never in my wildest speculation considered having mine end but here it was. On reflection, I have to assess that she made the right decision for both of us. Not that either of us were bad people, we were just bad together. After a healing period, we would become close friends right up until her too early death from cancer in 2012.

71. The House at Fraser & 21st.

The next few years were a bit of a wasteland for me in some ways. I was never 'one of the boys', I loved the ladies – still do. It is not that I was deliberately unkind, careless, or disrespectful, I was just emotionally absent. I apologize to all the lovely ladies I met during this time. I hope they went on to live wonderful lives. They all deserved better then I could offer them.

Being ever practical, the apartment that I had on Cardero Street in Vancouver's West End was too expensive for me to keep up on my own. I answered an ad to share a house with a couple of lads. The house was just east of Fraser Street on 21st Avenue. I went for an interview and was grilled by this English chap whom I must have impressed enough to offer me a room. The other roommate was also an expat Brit. He was a very reserved, blond, good-looking guy from London. He had done his apprenticeship in ladies hairdressing in London before immigrating to Canada in 1965. Over the course of the next several months, Tom and I became good friends. He being the ultra-reserved, private person he was, it took that long. The effort was worth it for me anyway and we are still pals so many years later.

The third person, Keith, my inquisitor, left the house to move with his wife to be, back to Australia. To fill the third seat, I brought in a friend of mine by the name of John Linnell. John and I met a couple of years earlier when I was visiting a girl friend at her dwelling in an apartment house. While there, I heard a guitar being played through the paper-thin walls. I knocked on the door and introduced myself to this tall, enigmatic, Welshman. He turned out to be a consummate philosopher. We chatted about music and life and I talked him into giving me some guitar lessons. I played my best rendition of House of the Rising Sun for him. He was suitably unimpressed but took me on anyway. As it turned out, John would be suitably unimpressed but tolerant of me, and my musical ability for the next forty years or so.

John moved into the house. I forgot to mention that he was blind as a bat. Well, not quite. He had what he described as some peripheral vision which we learned meant that he could in perfect light make out shapes. He had an amazing ability to get around using his superb memory capacity. Once he had walked around a room, he would know where every chair, door, and even ashtray was. A few people in my life are so important for the fact that they always had the ability to cut through my BS and challenge my fiber and intellect. John is one of these.

The house was a great party house and we had some wild ones. We also spent some great afternoons just sitting around drinking beer and yakking. One time a bunch of us were watching a charity telethon when an advertisement for skydiving came on. Like a twit, I said 'why don't we do that'. Before I could say 'pull my rip-cord', we were out in Chilliwack training for our first jump. Tom, Leo, and I. Now I am terrified of heights, I don't even like being a fraction less than six feet! This goes way back to the days when I went window cleaning with my Dad. He always had to do the high stuff because it would take me forever to complete one windowpane while hanging on to the ladder for dear life. So, here we were listening to this ever so British instructor detailing the finer points of surviving after leaving the aircraft at five thousand feet. It was all a bit of a blur to me. I vaguely recall after a tumultuous takeoff in a tiny Cessna, thinking that I would rather jump than land with this Kamikaze nut of a pilot.

At the given time I climbed out of the right hand door and perched with my left foot on a four-inch wide peg, while holding on to the under the wing strut. Our instructor had told us that at the appropriate time he would tap on our leg to indicate that it was time to go. Right. He whacked the back of my knee so hard that I was hurled into the stratosphere trying to remember my count, and ripcord procedure.

Once the parachute mercifully opened there was a few minutes of utter bliss, a weightless floating sensation with no feeling of downward movement. This temporary euphoria was rudely interrupted when I discovered an urgent need to recall the procedure for landing in water. The instructor had covered this but in the context that it was his duty, though not to worry as the river was five miles away. Well, from 4,000 feet the Fraser River was right there between my curling toes. I did miss the river and other than spraining my ankle on landing, survived to tell.

72. McKim: This also needs a book.

A couple of months after moving in with the boys, I got a call from Joff who in the meantime had gone from his job at the print shop to take up a position as Production Manager for a very prestigious advertising agency. Now however, he was planning to go into business with brother Jurgen and was given the task of recommending his own replacement. He asked if I would be interested. As it happened, my boss had finally turned down my business proposal and though his reasons were sound enough, I was truly disappointed. So, when Joff's offer came out of the blue I did not hesitate and met Frank Anfield the branch manager, the following day. We had a very good meeting, I liked him right away, and he hired me there and then, so I suppose it was mutual. Frank was an ultra conservative, always suited in dark blue with a light blue buttoned down shirt. He was a big man and wore large spectacles that he would peer over at times giving himself a very venerable appearance. He became a most trusted associate, mentor and friend.

My title was Production Manager of McKim Benton & Bowles and I was responsible for producing advertisements, radio and TV commercials and a slew of printed materials from billboards to brochures. I was the agency Purchasing Agent. My role was similar to that of a movie producer, (as opposed to a movie director). I did the budgeting and hiring of all materials and services that went into producing the creative product. I loved it. I started work June 15, 1971 the same day as a man by the name of Bev Machesney who would go on to be the next branch manager and my Bridge partner for the next forty-odd years.

At the agency, we worked like hell but lived like kings. From day one through the next thirty-five years or so, I worked an average of nine to ten-hour days plus weekends if needed. There were perks however. We rarely bought a lunch, never paid for a theatre ticket or hockey game. Our sponsors were the media department and our suppliers. Now in my defence of this payola, I should say that I never accepted a free lunch from anyone with whom I was not actually conducting business. I was always 'on-call' and since a lot of serious business decision and instruction took place on the bond of a verbal handshake, it had great import to know the people I dealt with. We were known and welcomed at all the fine restaurants and shown to the best tables. It was quite wonderful – kind of like being a 'Good Fellow' without the blood.

Vancouver in the 70s was still only a large town with none of the negatives associated with a 'city'. I would walk down the main streets in the business district and know most of the people I passed at least by sight. I had my own taxi account and used it as needed, even to get me home after a Friday night Scotch club gathering. These events were ad-hoc and took place on some Fridays after a particularly hectic week. The revelers would chip in to get a bottle of Scotch from the nearby liquor store and then we would kill it between lively conversations.

When I joined McKim, our digs were in the Burrard Building, which was *the* place to be in the early 70s. It was strategically located at Georgia & Burrard, just next door to the Ritz pub where we often wrote and designed ads, did storyboards, and now and again, even had lunch. The next couple of years I employed every bit of knowledge that I had gleaned from being in the printing business in my job as a producer, adding experience to my knowledge as I went. Not having had much in the way of formal education, I figured if I outworked anyone with whom I came into contact, I would prevail – and I did.

There were two significant aspects of the world of McKim. The first was that we had an amazing assembly of talent at all positions and levels. Just about all of the people I worked with during these ten years went on to have first-rate careers and I would bounce off many of them as I went along my own career path. They were clever – no brilliant. They worked like crazy to excel and exceed all expectations from both clients and employers.

The second factor was that they were certifiably nuts. In the 2000s TV series *MadMen* it shows a glimmer of what life was like in the Ad business, in the 70s, but it only shows one aspect of it, that being the 'fooling around'. Oh sure we had lots of that, but of much more interest were the characters. Man, I mean right off the wall. You could write an episode or two on any one of dozens of people that I worked with.

Changing the names to protect my literary ass from suit, here are a few samples.

Our art directors were probably the wackiest. Cid was six-foot, five-inches of nuts. For a time it is said that he hid from his creditors by moving into his office and it was common to arrive in the morning to the aroma of bacon and eggs. His cohort was John, 5'1" in Chelsea boots. He looked so straight but after just one sniff of a barmaid's apron became an absolute barbarian. He flipped his lid one time while we were having lunch at Charlie Brown's, because the barman mistakenly called him Cid! 'There's nearly two feet difference in height' he yelled while standing on the top of our table 'I'll kill that man'.

There was the Oz. Never saw him eat a single morsel; he was convinced that there was every needed kind of nutrition in a few pints of beer. He used to take his drawing pad and felt markers down to the Ritz pub and work from his 'regular' table. I once saw him complete the layouts for an entire season for Park & Tilford Distillers during an extended lunch session. And it was great stuff too. Frank and my pal JC sold the campaign that very day.

Among our account guys were a pair of real ass bandits. There favourite reason for not being in the office when the boss or their wives called was that they were at the 'Y'. They had figured out that giving the impression of keeping in shape benefited both employer and spouse alike. Yeah, well, they kept in shape all right.

In those days, we had a 'typing pool' as none of us could type. The young women we employed were technically for the purpose of doing our correspondence, but in reality it seems they were also hired to look wonderful and provide visual compensation for the ludicrously long days that were worked. One such nubile was Doreen. I recall poor Jack almost swallowing his glove just to stop himself from drooling when she walked past his office one morning in her oversized glasses and undersized sweater. His buddy, a supplier of ours was no better and once broke his arm jumping out of a bedroom window escaping from a too early returning husband.

It was not just the boys. Our female-dominated Media department was knick-named 'The Wild Bunch' for their high-octane lunches, Scotch in the desk drawer, and pot in the washroom.

We had a receptionist who charmed and seduced any man she set her mind to, and she could have taken a run at them all, from senior executives to the mailman. I believe she also may have sold watches, jewellery, and illicit substances from the front desk. We thought she was great. My suppliers were happily kept waiting for me if I was trapped in a meeting.

There really are just too many stories to visit them all but I will do my personal favourite. Very early one morning I was alone in the office as I often was, when the phone rang. The caller had a strong accent, maybe eastern European. He insisted that I should give him a slogan for his new welding company. After trying several times to explain that we were a full service advertising agency and that we just did not work that way, all the while listening to his insistence that "You's are the guys's to do this". Finally, I said, "Hang on a moment. Ok, here it is, *All's weld that ends weld*". There was dead silence at the other end of the phone. I thought he had hung up. Then he spoke.

"I like it" he said, "How much is that"?

"Three Hundred Dollars" I said.

"I'll take it" he replied, and believe it or not, sent me a cheque – made out to me of course.

To my compatriots, I salute you one and all. I went to McKim as a boy with a past and would leave as a man with a future.

I was feeling really good about myself at this time. A great job that I loved and in which I was well paid and respected, it was time to give something back. I had tried to be an unofficial 'big brother' to a friend's fatherless nephew without a great deal of success, but thought the concept was sound. I started to check the Big Brothers organization and subsequently signed on. After the interviews and background checks the scary day arrived when I sat in a small office and they brought in my 'little brother'. My fear was, what if I disliked him on first sight? Well, that did not happen, and Brett and I had a very worthwhile ten years together. I saw him once a week and took him away on many weekends. He still calls me from time to time to ask how I am doing.

Our branch of McKim grew very rapidly both in size and prestige. There were just twelve of us when I joined and we would be sixty-five when I left ten-years later. These years – the McKim years would be the most formative, enjoyable, and rewarding working years of my working life.

73. Meanwhile, back at the Ranch.

Beaverdam Guest Ranch had become an integral part of my life. From Easter Weekend right through Thanksgiving I would make the four and a half hour drive up through the Fraser Canyon to the ranch every weekend. The ranch was a microcosm of a small town. It was a living soap opera in which I made some neat friends from among the regular guests. As wrangler and general entertainer I got to spend time with all those who came up for the week, or just weekends, among them was Doctor Frank. Doc was a G.P. in North Vancouver but had a passion for riding that he satiated by driving his horse trailer all the way up to Clinton with his two horses. He and wife Carol were regulars and I enjoyed his company a lot. Through Frank, I met another couple that became regulars, Vera and Mike Brundage, both of whom were patients and friends of his. Vera was a life of the party kind of gal, outgoing, vivacious and with limitless energy. She did not drink and did not need it to be the life and soul of our evening gatherings. Her husband Mike was one big sun of gun, slow talking with a terrifically irreverent sense of humour. All of us got along really well, so much so that we began to socialize in Vancouver as well as at the ranch.

Imagine how thrilled and more than a bit envious I was when I found out that Doc & Carol, Mike & Vera, and Vera's parents Lou & Vic, had formed a partnership and bought the ranch from the Federspiels'! They all sold their Vancouver homes and moved lock stock and barrel onto the ranch. Doc and Carol took the main ranch house, Mike, and Vera with their two boys, and Vic and Lou with their two still at home girls and a boy moved into respective trailers on the property. How about them apples!

I got quite involved with them in the early days, helping with their advertising and promotion. I took no pay, as indeed I never did for any of the other contributions I made to the ranch. It was enough that they gave me room and board, covered my gas expenses, and put a saddle under me any time I wanted it. Not to mention the smorgasbord provided by the constant supply of new and nubile guests.

Now I should perhaps mention in case I forgot to earlier that the ranch was a lot like the notion of Vegas today, 'what goes to the ranch stays at the ranch'. Combine this with the fact that females outnumber the males at guest ranches by better than two to one, and you have the makings of Shangri-La from the male point of view. You also have a very vigorous environment with lots of machismo, sun, skin, and alcohol resulting in anything goes. Some of the shenanigans need another book and a non-de plume in order to give details. It was all a blast. One long weekend I had three girlfriends show up, none of them knew about the others. I must have lost ten pounds in three days.

74. Lynda.

Because of the quick and steady growth of McKim Vancouver, we had to move the offices and chose a very modern building complex called the Bentall Centre. I was the architect of the move, which was a thankless, hairy undertaking trying to keep fifty 'A' type personalities happy. On the day of the move, after giving up a Saturday and working all day moving stuff in, so that everybody would be ready to resume work early on the Monday morning, I found myself walking to the elevator at the same time as one of the young female employees.

We all had secretaries in those days as it would be several more years before most senior employees learned to type or use a computer. We used either Dictaphones or wrote longhand to communicate with junior female staff members who would then type the letter or report and present it for signature. It was no accident that all these girls were not only capable but also quite lovely. If management wanted the senior staff to work ridiculous hours it made sense to have an attractive environment and sexist as this was, it seemed to work pretty well, and I never heard either side complain. Anyway the young lady that I found myself chatting to while waiting for the elevator was our diminutive, and wonderful Office Services person by the name of Lynda Gibb. Now in her job, she filled in for just about every other support position in the company from secretary to receptionist to event planner to art filing. Did I say art filing? I did, and that is what she did for my department as well as typing reports for me from time to time. Lynda had the tiniest frame and gorgeous thick dark brown hair that cascaded down way beyond her small waist. Her brown eyes reflected her ever present smile and happy disposition.

Now I had never seriously considered Lynda as anything other than a nice co-worker as I really thought her to be far to young for me. She was probably twenty-one, but could easily have passed for seventeen. I on the other hand, was a once-married veteran of the gender wars. But anyway, as we descended in the elevator I was thanking her for all the help in getting my stuff filed away and without much forethought asked if she would like a lift home. It was a beautiful warm May evening so we took a drive around the famous and beautiful Stanley Park, and sat on the grass overlooking Second Beach. It was nice.

We met a few more times and began seeing each other on a regular though nonexclusive bases.

It was clear to me from the onset that this was different. I was determined that we would either be just good friends or something much, much more. It was not going to be anything in between. As it turned out it would be all of these things.

In the beginning, I wanted to distance this relationship from those in my recent and current life. I did not even kiss her goodnight for about three months, She probably thought me weird. When I did get around to it, she laughed – most disconcerting. This was not a usual response to my attentions.

Then I lost my driving license.

One of the on the job hazards of driving five hundred miles every weekend with purpose, was the inevitable traffic tickets. I drove a 1966 Mustang convertible – Red with black top, up through the switchbacks of the Fraser Canyon. This car with its 289cu in V8 engine, in a light body really could fly. I knew the canyon road so well I could see way ahead and could tell if there was anything going into a curve from the other direction and therefore could overtake on bends when it looked like I was risking driving into the oncoming traffic. Or so I thought anyway. I also played the odds in that I hoped the Mounties either were busy ticketing another driver or were having a doughnut or something when I roared by. If they gave chase I would sometimes out run them depending on which stretch of road I was on. There was not that many patrol cars out on this highway so radioing ahead was not always an option for them. Unfortunately, the odds were stacked, and via the mail, I did receive a total of twenty-one points on my record before getting hauled into court and having my license extracted from me. The punishment was a fine and a three-month driving ban that would be extended until I had successfully completed a defensive driving course.

Up went another notch in my relationship with the lovely Lynda. In order to feed my passion(s), I had to have someone drive me up to the ranch on weekends. Yep, you've guessed it, Lynda. In fact, she actually took over my car, which, ended up being the give away that Lynda and I were indeed an item. A friend Nancy, who put two and two together and actually did manage to come up with four, saw her.

Amazingly, we had managed to keep our relationship a secret from our fellow workers for a couple of years. This was done in part because we did not want the gossip, and in part because I still really did feel like the dirty old man going out with this lovely sheltered young girl.

75. The Spring roundup and the Rodeo.

One of the great annual events took place in the early spring. The southern Cariboo is a vast area of ranch land and at this time included the biggest cattle ranch in North America called The Gang Ranch. The area we were in abuts this impressive piece of property to its east. Our area is comprised of several smaller cattle-raising outfits. These ranches share certain services and pool their resources to serve the common good. The cattle and to some extent the horses are let loose through the winter months to fend for their selves.

A Range Rider employed by the collective Cattlemen's Association, patrols the whole area, keeps an eye in them, and makes sure there is no undue distress. He keeps the ranchers informed as to where the herds are so that regular feed can be distributed in the bad weather when foraging is impossible.

I got to know the Range Rider, Alvin Kerr and his wife Helen, quite well over the years, and went out with him on several occasions, riding long days in the saddle. He and his wife were tiny people who rode huge horses. It always amazed me the ease with which they swung up onto the saddle. Part of their job in the early spring was to keep an eye on the calving.

Come April, all the ranchers got together for the annual roundup. This entailed locating all the livestock and driving them from their winter pastures to a massive collection of corrals at Big Bar Ranch. Here, the herds would be separated by brands ensuring that the respective calves stayed with their branded mothers. What happened next is just part of cowboy life but sounds and is quite violent. A calf is de-horned, castrated, and branded all in the space of about three minutes. It is a wonder they don't die of shock. I am sure any one of those would take care of me! I never did rise to the caliber of cowhand to perform any of these functions. My job was to help in moving the cattle from place to place and generally assist the real cowboys on their cutting horses. I have ridden a cutting horse but only in an arena as a sport. This is a superb team of man and horse whose job it is to separate a single cow (and calf) from the herd. Once the rider has identified the cow and pointed the horse at it, the horse takes over and all the cowboy has to do is stay in the saddle – no mean feat. The first time I tried it I wanted to look cool and keep both hands away from the saddle. Bad move. Even cowboys hold on to the horn in this process. I ended up with a bad hematoma from knee to essentials.

After the long days work the cooking fires would be started and the parting began. Now though we call them all cowboys, most of the hands were in fact Indians. We had a super time at these events and we were tolerated, even welcome up to a point. We drank our beer and ate our fair share of 'prairie oysters' aka calves nuts, but at a certain time of the late evening a friend from the other side of the tracks would advise us that it was time to head out. We did.

One of the interesting aspects of Canadian history is actually that it is so recent. This makes it very tangible, you feel you can reach out and touch it. I have visited with original pioneers of this country, and their families: the Grinders, Caldwells, Hellers and Pigeons, all were important contributors to our rich pioneering history. My friend Mike's eldest son married into the Pigeon family tying his family in perpetuity to Canadian history.

Another great annual event was the Clinton Rodeo. Clinton was, and still is on the Canadian professional rodeo circuit. Theirs is held the weekend after the much larger and posher version at Cloverdale. To call Clinton's a 'professional' event was a stretch in those days, though they did get some first rate riders who followed the circuit and enjoyed the country rodeos that were held in lots of small cowboy towns throughout the Canadian west. Some of us entered the rodeo in a couple of events, the first being 'Milking a wild Cow'. This is a team event in which you and a buddy get in the coral with a cow, very wild off the range, and have to fill a small bottle about the size of a shot glass with its milk. Sound easy? Try it, but not at home, and certainly not sober. The other event was the downhill, now outlawed as a danger to man and beast. The contestants would gather on a hill above the Rodeo grounds and at the sound of the gun, leap into the great yonder like the *Man from Snowy River*. My favourite for this event was a monster of a buckskin by the name of Limbo. He was something else, never faltered. That horse could, and sometimes did, walk through trees and barbed wire fences.

Now as time went by it became clear that Carol, the Doc's wife was not all that happy. We did not know why, and Doc's explanation was that she suffered from depression. I had no experience with depression at all so I suppose I just took his word for it. She would show up at the evening get together and just sit in a corner with a strange smile on her face for the entire evening. Very odd. She also began to lament, and bend anyone's ear that would listen to her, that Frank was fooling around. Frank explained this all by saying it was all due to her condition and he was giving her medication for it.

Well guess what? We all were thinking poor Carol and her wacky imagination until one day the lovely and vivacious Vera and Dr. Frank bought a house in Clinton and left the ranch to move into it. Now you might think that this was all a disaster, and perhaps it was for Carol who seemed to get the worst of it. Vera and Doc were happy. He set up shop as the town G.P.; his shingle read Hickory, Dickory, Doc. Vera had a beautiful home and very soon a delightful flower garden. Her younger son moved in with them. Mike and son Wayne stayed on at the ranch with the Scott family and became an eligible bachelor. He would eventually team up with the beautiful nubile Dani and they would have two children and a long life together. Vera and Doc visited regularly and joined the weekend parties. I would play guitar and sing rock n' roll songs with my partner John Linnell. My buddy Leo would spread his gregarious nature and provide fun and entertainment for kids, dogs, and adults alike.

It was a wonderful era. We would ride all day, eat and drink our faces off and party all night only to begin again the next morning. I would not try this at home either. I have led trail rides out with over sixty guests. If you have never taken part in a full out cavalry charge with that many horses you will have no idea what a rush that is. It feels like there are hundreds of you. I would find a favourite wide meadow and string everyone out in a skirmish line and start at a walk, then a trot, then a controlled lope that finally break out into a full gallop for over a quarter of a mile. All you can hear is the thunder of hooves, the squeak of leather and the snorting of animals. Not the most sensible nor safest thing in the world to do, but hey, I never said I was perfect. In later years, I did learn a bit more respect for the animals. After the charge we rounded up all the rider-less horses, extracted guests from water hazards and trees and make our way back to the ranch with heads full of stories to tell future grandchildren.

76. THE HOUSE BREAKS UP. THE FOLKS VISIT.

By now my housemate Tom had moved out. He took up with a workmate of his from the hairdressing saloon and eventually moved in with her. Sue was a beautiful, healthy looking, athletic, smart Aussie (if that is not a contradiction of terms). We all took to her right away and we would share many, many, good times together in the years to come. They would be good friends to us and wonderful role models to our children.

I had moved out of the house and was living in a nice, large, though boxy apartment in Kitsilano. It was 1972. Mum and Dad planned to come out for a visit in the summer. I was thrilled. Now my possessions were to say the least meager. I had one of those small foldout box stereo/tape-decks, a bed, a knife fork, spoon, and an electric frying pan. Lynda suggested that I might want to expand a little before my folks arrived. As it happened, a friend of her Mum and Dad was selling some furniture. In no time flat I had a four-seat chesterfield with matching chair, a coffee and two end tables, and a lovely red woven rug. Hey, I had arrived. But Lynda was not finished. In short, order she had me get a kitchen table, chairs, and set of plates and cutlery. Now we were ready for Ron & Nell.

It is amazing to me that they came over. I helped with their fare of course as indeed I sent money home from the day I got my first job in Canada until after all my children were born. They still had to come up with a lot of cash. I could not wait to show them around my new country. I had a 1966 Mustang convertible in which I buzzed them to all the tourist sites in and around Vancouver. Lynda came with us.

On one of these day trips, I mentioned that we would be going away for a few days to visit the ranch, Banff, and Jasper. Mum said to Lynda 'Why don't you come'. She immediately accepted Mum's offer and quickly arranged for vacation time from McKim. Off we went.

The first night was kind of interesting. We pulled into a motel in Salmon Arm, a small town in the BC lake district of the Okanagan. We booked two rooms and unpacking the bags, Mum placed her and Lynda's bags in front of her room. I picked up Lynda's bag and moved it over to mine. That was it, not a word was said but it was likely a shock. We all had a super trip though. After doing the Rockies, we ended up back at the Ranch where Mum and Dad were treated like royalty. I got them both onto horses and gave them lasting memories and stories to take back to Cuckfield. This would prove to be the first of so many trips to Canada for my folks. They hit it off right away with Lynda's parents Grace and Jim, so much so that we almost had to get married. Over the next twenty-five years, our parents would visit with each other on both sides of the Atlantic. They went to France, Scotland, and Wales together on subsequent trips – without us.

77. The Great Trek.

One early morning leaving Leo's place after a night of partying I noticed that Lynda was not her usual happy self. I pulled over and asked what was up. In her own way, she laid out for me that we were at a stage in our relationship where I had to shit or get off the pot. Ever practical, she saw our relationship as an investment and wanted to know just how much effort was worth her while. If I just wanted to keep going as we were, so be it, but she would feel free to keep her options open. Wow! I went home that night with a lot to think about. Since my breakup with Ethel, I had to admit to myself that I had not been a particularly nice person in regards to girl friends. I did not set out to intentionally hurt any one else's feelings but not having many of my own, there was no doubt that I had. What Lynda was telling me was that she was not willing to ride that train. We either move it forward or she might just get off. This was a huge shock to me. I knew that the reality of moving anywhere without her was intolerable. I smartened up.

In the spring of 1974 Tom and Sue tied the knot. Come summer, my buddy Leo was contemplating his upcoming 30th birthday and we were thinking of what we might do to celebrate. There is not that many good books written on the history of the Cariboo country, which is a shame because there is great colour and adventure contained there in. A couple of submissions worth a read are *The Cariboo Cowboy* by Harry Marriott and *Grass beyond the*

Mountains by Richard Hobson. Harry died in the early sixties not long after his book came out but I met his wife Peg, when she lived out at Big Bar Lake. Some days if we had a smallish group, I would take the ride out that way and pop in for tea on her porch. She loved the company and that is more than she did Harry. She was a feisty little woman and having been born and raised in the Cariboo had wonderful stories to tell about the birth of the cattle business in Western Canada. She was the local school-ma'am in Hat Creek when she met Harry who though an English emigrant from 1905 was by then a seasoned cowman. Peg Marriott lived in Clinton till her death in 2008 at the grand age of one hundred and seven.

Hobson's book took the cattle industry's story, one step further and into the Chilcotins. This book really stirred something in me. Having spent so much time in ranch country, I relished everything about it: its land, its people, and its history. This book is about what in my mind was the North American Cattlemen's last frontier. It talks about the vast area in British Columbia that stretches north from The Cariboo to the Itcha Mountains and west from Williams Lake to Bella Coola and the fjords of the Pacific coast. This is a massive pristine plateau of fresh air and grasslands. The pioneers went where few white men had ever been, establishing settlements such as Alexis Creek, Tatla Lake, Nimpo Lake and the fabulous Anahiem Lake. The richness and historical importance of this area really is under-documented. It is said that the last known Indian massacre in Canada took place on the Blackwater River in early 1864. Just imagine, this is only one hundred years prior to my setting foot on Canadian soil. This incident in the wars was between the white road builders and the local Tsilhqot'in (Chilcotin) people, resulted in fourteen men employed by Alfred Waddington dead. Five warriors thought responsible, were tricked into surrendering under a truce agreement, tried, and hanged.

I love English history for its colour and breadth. I enjoy Canadian history for its closeness.

So, when Leo got my input as to what we might do for his birthday we soon settled on a trip through the afore mentioned Chilcotins. We packed his GMC Jimmy with tents and camping gear, plus eighteen cases of beer, as there was an impending strike by the BC Liquor Control Board workers, which meant closed liquor stores (no wonder I have such disdain for unions).

Our plan was to be gone for two weeks starting out from Beaverdam, heading north to Williams Lake and then west to the coast to pick up a freighter that would take us back to Vancouver. The paved road finished just out of Williams Lake as it crossed the Fraser River. What lay ahead was over two hundred miles (as the crow flies), of at best dirt track.

We stopped the first night at Alexis Creek to visit the son of a printing rep friend of mine. Don Brecknock was a guide outfitter and came with horses, a jet boat, and floatplane. We stayed for several days exploring and fishing wilderness lakes for three to four-pound Rainbow Trout. It was fantastic. Leo had his birthday there but was so ticked off about turning thirty that he did not drink all day – no really. The rest of our trip lived up to and exceeded our expectations and we arrived in Bella Coola in one piece in spite of having to lower the truck down a semi-washed out road on a precipitous incline, using ropes.

Bella Coola is a First Nations fishing village. There were hardly any white folks to be seen. Leo and I went to a dance at the village hall and after 9:30 I thought it best we got our arses out of there. He was so depressed at the lack of action he phoned his girlfriend Laura who had been angling for some time to get a marriage license in order not to be shipped back to Australia, and asked her to marry him.

Sadly, Leo would have too many bad relationships out of which he ended up making a lot of unfortunate lifestyle choices. Almost forty years later, I would hold his hand as he reached for the Great Hall – Valhalla.

78. I BUILD A NEST – FOR TWO.

Lynda, in her own subtle and ever-practical way had encouraged me to get out of the renting nonsense and buy a place. This I did and was now living in my own apartment on 5th Avenue in the hippy capitol of Western Canada called Kitsilano. By this time, she and I were in fact exclusive. We even talked about moving in together as was the on-going trend of the day but I felt it would be too upsetting for her family and I did not want to offend these nice people. So, one late August evening just after we got back from a trip, Lynda and I were in my apartment when I happened to mention that perhaps we should just get married. I picked up the phone and asked her Dad to have lunch with me the following day. We met at one of my favourite mid-day haunts called Charlie Browns where I officially asked for Lynda's hand. Well before you could say 'what time is the flight out of here'; we were married on October 26, 1974, two weeks before my 30th birthday.

We had a very modest wedding. I had no money – I did not even buy Lynda an engagement ring. I really think on reflection that Lynda was gypped. None of my family came out to our wedding but my close friends, who, as with most emigrants are in effect family, were all there. I booked Lynda and me into a motel for the night close to where the reception was going to be. It turned out to be very lower sleaze – the Sportsman Motel on Kingsway. Lynda had not been consulted on this and I packed an over-night bag for her. I quickly learned that a Moo-Moo was not an ideal choice. But hey, we were heading off to Hawaii the following day.

Our honeymoon was not great for Lynda. She was very sick. I was actually thinking of giving her back to her mother when we got home. Thankfully, this did not happen. I loved Hawaii. The wonderful fragrance of the Plumeria flowers that formed the leys that greeted us at the airport to me is an indelible memory. The warm waters in which I snorkeled to watch abundant and colourful fish, and the romantic sunsets watched to the sounds of Hawaii were all perfection.

Tom, Louise, Lynda, Ron, Leo, Margaret.

I tried surfing. There I was a quarter of a mile off Waikiki Beach with about two hundred surfers – all waiting expectantly for the 'right wave'. Several waves came and went with hardly a murmur from the crowd. Then. The whole line quivered with anticipation, and all started to paddle like crazy, me included. Well, off went one hundred and ninety nine skimming bodies leaving me breathless and paddling in their wake. I didn't get it. A few moments later something under the water brushed past my lonely leg. I hit the beach at about forty knots.

79. Dad has a heart attack.

A year after our wedding, Dad suffered a heart attack just before his 60th birthday. He survived but his window cleaning days were over. He and Mum had swapped houses with sister Chris and Ted so that they could buy Number 11. At least it kept this mystical address in the family for a few more years. They then moved into a 'granny suite' attached to sister Ellen and Roy's house in Bolney. Unfortunately, Mum would never settle there or anywhere else for that matter. She hated and feared the isolation of this lovely but remote farmhouse.

Dad did find a new job working in Burgess Hill for a manufacturing company. He loved it. The firm and its employees all really appreciated him for his work ethic and good humour.

Continuing his philanthropic work, he visited the sick and lonely and did is own 'meals on wheels' thing. Mum prepared extra meals that Dad would deliver to people that he knew were either not eating properly or just that they were on their own. I do not know how she did it really with her small income but there always seemed to be an extra potato in the pot when needed.

Dad loved his cards and played regularly at the Silver Threads Club in the village spreading cheer, and companionship while cheating at crib and whist. Hell, he even cheated himself at solitaire.

80. HERE COMES MARTY. THEN CHRISTOPHER.

Ron, Martin and Supernan (Gibb).

I guess I must have mentioned to Lynda one day that we should find a bigger place, a two-bedroom apartment perhaps? Always the forward thinker, when I came home from Bridge the following day, Lynda had a house picked out – bugger an apartment. She dragged me down to see it that night and we bought it right there and then. We moved in to our nice little house in Kitsilano, just in time. 1976 was the year that while driving down through the United States, Lynda confirmed what she had suspected - she was going to have a baby. Three thousand miles of morning sickness and another seven months produced a beautiful healthy boy. We called him Martin Pelham after his maternal Great Grandfather and his hereditary family name. Lynda and I were absolutely delighted. In spite of nearly forty years of Colic, Marty is an adventure well worth the trip.

For the next two years I probably took our little house to the dump – twice. We painted, renovated, and put two sleeping-rooms and a bathroom in the basement to get some income. Other then the excitement of having pot-smoking pyromaniacs, and psychiatric patients in our house, it worked out rather well?

Without a lot of preamble, the house next door to Lynda's parents became available. This was a large four-bedroom dwelling in the very respectable neighbourhood of Point Grey. The price was right but we were rather stretched for spare cash so I borrowed a down payment from Lynda's parents so we could buy the place. I rented it out at a profit, for more then the cost of payments for about a year, in which time the values had increased an appreciable amount. We than sold the Kits house and I paid Lynda's parents back all the money I had borrowed – with interest.

We have lived next door to my in-laws for nearly forty years and for a lot of that time it was very special to have them part of our and our children's lives. The have been very generous.

The Circle H guest ranch.

We moved into the big house just in time as it turned out, as we went back into the diaper business with the advent of a baby boy who in birth seemed to take forever to come out. He was so long. A truly nice person from the day he was born, forever. We called him Christopher Bute. He never failed to show the character of the fine man he would become.

81. WEST GRAPHIKA/KARO.

By this time I was on McKim's Board of Directors, an aspiration in which I took great pride, as it was not usual for a Production Manager to rise to that level in an advertising agency. The promotion came at a price however as directors were expected to be shareholders. Off to the bank I went and took out a huge loan. Scared the heck out of me. At almost exactly the same time as this my friend Don was investing in his company. We both went out to 'lunch' to contemplate what we had done - and had the good sense to go straight home afterwards, not back to the office.

Difficult though this investment was to deal with at the time, I would never live to regret it.

After holding this position for a few years, my problem became what to do next. My skill and experience was in company administration and graphic production. The fact that this was within a marketing company did not make me a marketer. That is a quite different discipline and career path. Due to a natural acumen for finance, I became a favourite of our Comptroller at head office in Toronto who was in-line to move up to company treasurer. He and I had become directors on the same day. I had a knack for maximizing profitability. By the pragmatic application of legitimate creative fees I produced more revenue from this, than from production commissions. As this was not the case in our head office, I think he wanted me to consider a move. This would have meant going to Toronto, and I quickly learned that the only way Lynda would ever leave Point Grey, Vancouver, is in a pine box.

All through my McKim years, one of my principal suppliers was Joff's company – West Graphika. They took our print advertising concepts from felt-marked drawings and manuscript, to typeset graphic assembly ready for the camera-work that would prepare the material for publication. This was a huge part of our business.

Now as it happens McKim was in an expansion mode in which it was investing in 'supply' companies such as recording studios, public relation firms, and looking at graphic art studios. This became an opportunity. After a long courtship, I sold my shares in McKim and purchased a position in West Graphika, joining them as Vice President and General Manager in 1981.

This maneuver was one of my few financial coups. With the funds that I got from McKim, I paid off my mortgage. I then took out a new mortgage to buy the West Graphika stock. All interest on this loan was tax deductable and with interest rates as high as 12.5% this was quite a benefit. As I say, investing was never a strong suit for me. I was either, too stupid too busy or too scared to make money. I gained wealth the old fashioned way – I saved – month by month, year by year, eggcup by eggcup. We never bought anything we could not pay cash for. We did not do lattés, meals out or buy toys; all the time we were raising our family. And never did I pay one cent of credit card interest in my entire life.

One of the in-going criterion for my going to West Graphika was that Joff, for whom I had the greatest respect, was getting involved with all kinds of investments and would be less involved with the running of the company. This never quite happened as his outside interests spluttered requiring him to stay in the firm to make a living. This set up the possibility of a clash. I never was able to acquire his visioning talent, and he would never contend with my pragmatic approach to cost justification. Towards the end of our ten-years together, our industry went through some dramatic changes, which I would say were equal to the invention of movable type in their implications.

The Apple Macintosh and Adobe.

Almost over-night our principal income, that of supplying custom typesetting was challenged by every designer and art-director who could, or learned, to operate a computer. Our original designed type-fonts that cost as much as four hundred dollars each, now had an albeit inferior rendition available from Adobe for twenty-nine each. The pressure this put on our operation was totally debilitating. I had to downsize in a hurry, which meant having to let staff members go, some of whom I had known and worked with for almost two decades. This was one of the worst periods of my working life, causing me to walk the floors all night long before each and every move.

The company now tried to morph into a more comprehensive design firm by adding industrial design and branding. As part of this change we became KARO design resources.

Jurgen, Joff's brother and senior partner, went through some changes in his life that resulted in him leaving the company. This did not last however, I'm not sure why, perhaps he lost his other interests. Anyway, he returned and brought with him a girlfriend. Though a very good designer she was very expensive in her use of our in-house services putting pressure on our already troubled profitability. She and I did not get along.

One day we happened to be in the parking lot at the same time and got into an argument in which she became very heated, screaming at me in fact. When I came back from lunch Joff in effect fired me. I take some responsibility for this in that I put him in a position from which he had no easy exit. I believe Jurgen may have given him an ultimatum that either I go or Jurgen would. This, for Joff was no contest in the final analysis.

One of the saddest parts for me was that no one came to my rescue. I hired most of the people in the company and to a large extent was instrumental in establishing their careers. In tough times I was also the hatchet man and likely they never knew how I agonized over having to let people go. I perhaps unrealistically thought at the time that a bunch of people would rebel and strenuously object to my dismissal. Dumb.

I can't say I was not bitter at having been dumped because of one of Jurgen's popsys – I just had to try to deal with it and move on.

82. Always the dramatist: Susie.

While at West Graphika we had another joyful event. I was present at both boys' births. A frightening experience to say the least. I was quite naïve believe it or not, in the ways of the world and in no way prepared for the drama of a delivery room. I have no doubt that my face was whiter then my surgical mask. Thank God Lynda was such a quiet person. All around me there were thoroughly disconcerting howls from other birthing rooms, Lynda just breathed.

Our daughter's arrival was what you might call a bit different. Lynda had a few anomalies that caused her to go to St Paul's Hospital for observation three-months prior to her delivery date. The doctors at the hospital decided to transfer her to VGH, as that was the children's hospital at the time.

Lynda told me, and the new 'expert' doctor that she really thought she was getting the urge to deliver. The Doctor told her to relax as that was not going to happen right now. He should have listened. So should I. We carried on and in due course Lynda called for a bedpan so I nipped down stairs to grab a cup of java. As I re-entered the maternity ward all hell was breaking lose, there were doctors and nurses running in all directions. Lynda had quietly given birth, all by herself, into a bedpan.

What followed was a couple of months of not knowing if we had a daughter or not. She was in an incubator and would have 'good shifts' and 'bad shifts'. We would not know from one day to the next if we were relieved or devastated. My friend Don Ogden would meet me in the coffee shop opposite the hospital and help me prepare for the day – and whatever it would bring. I am eternally grateful for this friendship.

Thank God Susie eventually got hold of life, stabilized, and we brought our little girl home.

So, Susanne would keep her flair for the dramatic, and a very special place in my heart forever.

83. THE FAMILY.

Having a family has been the greatest privilege of my life. Lynda and I have never been deep thinking, soul searching, and navel gazing kinds of people. Not overtly anyway. It is not like we ever sat down and discussed each and every aspect of our lives together. Mostly we allowed instinct to rule. We developed roles and responsibilities through osmosis with the unfaltering confidence in each other's love and commitment. I joke about not telling her anything, sort of. What I mean is, I do not share negative emotions, and few such thoughts or acts. I am not advocating this approach to life is for everyone but I would find discussing every minute detail of how I/she feels at any given moment, monumentally burdensome, annoying, and ultimately depressing. Raising a family is no task for weaklings and we have had our fair share of challenges, but does the good outweigh the bad – you bet your ass.

We had our children sign up for everything and anything they wanted to try, and we supported their efforts. I drove the 'taxi' and bus. I coached soccer for about fifteen years on and off between my 'little brother' Brett's team, and those of my boys. Sometimes we were just cheerleading. It was fantastic, and over and gone all too soon.

Every year from age five or six, I took the boys away for a week on my own. We travelled all over BC, from the Rockies to Vancouver Island. We camped; moteled it, took boat rides, fished, swam, and rode horses. We also all drove the van, shared a beer, farted, and shot guns from the moving vehicle like a gun-ship. We crossed condemned bridges: at full speed, built rafts, and forded rivers.

Was I having fun? Are you kidding?

On one of our trips, while sitting on the front porch of the Circle H Ranch with my sons, in rode the old, and weathered Mr. Caldwell, a range rider, and one of the last of his kind. The Caldwell's were founders of the town of Jesmond in and around 1913. On another trip, my sons would also meet Floyd Grinder; no I did not make that name up, a huge mountain of a man and Indian as Cochise. On one of our bonding trips, we were visiting with another cowboy friend of mine when in came Floyd to join us for a cup of coffee. We were drinking beer but I never did see Floyd drink. Anyway, Christopher had just gotten his ear pierced and was wearing an earring. Not being a great talker, when Floyd spoke you kind of listened. He looked at me and said 'your boy isn't sure of what sort he is Ron'. We figured out that he was referring to Chris's earring. Well, I never saw that ring in his ear again for the rest of the trip, and when we went to a rodeo the following day where the afore mentioned Floyd was the Rodeo Marshal, Chris was eager to be seen cleansed of the appendaged adornment.

84. His Worship.

One of Dad's great achievements was to be elected Mayor of Cuckfield. This is an honorary award bestowed upon the person who raises the most money for charity over the period of one year. It is corruption of the finest kind as each vote costs money and people can vote as many times as they like. The Lord Mayor's Day is a community event.

The election night takes place at the village hall where last minute voters are coerced into parting with cash right up to the final bell. The votes are counted, a winner declared and the party is on. The following day there is a fancy-dress parade and lots of goodies for the children. Of course the real winners are all the local charities that this event supports. Several members of Dad's family would proudly follow in these footsteps: daughter, sons-in-law, nephew and niece.

85. THE RGROUP.

When I left KARO I took a couple of months to reorient myself and get into a job-searching mode. At this time Christopher had taken up playing Canadian Football and it created a nice diversion for me as I went wholeheartedly into this 'new sport'. It was great. I became the Club Registrar, game day announcer/commentator, driver and all around cheerleader. At the end of his four years with the club, I was honoured with the presentation of the club's Builder Award. In my acceptance speech I dedicated the award to my father who worked so much harder and longer for much less official recognition. He got the love and respect of all the people that were touched by him. Hmm, on second thoughts, it was enough for him.

As part of my job networking, my friend Lloyd told me that an old colleague of ours from back in the McKim days was looking for a GM for her young company. I applied and was hired. Two very talented females, one a designer and the other a writer owned this firm. They were specializing in the marketing of Real Estate developments.

I worked there for eleven turbulent years in which I had the pleasure of associating with a superb bunch of young people many of whom I continue to see regularly. But, though I really liked and admired the two principals, I found working for two women who to my mind could never seem to separate the business from the personal, very tiring. They hired me as a General Manager, what they really wanted was an Executive Administrator. Eventually, this is what they got, and I got out.

86. Boating and 'Camp'.

After horses, the next great outdoor passion in my life was boating. Lynda's brother Pete and I shared a boat for about twenty years, from around 1974 on. It was a seventeen-foot Fiberform with an outboard motor and trailer. We mostly trailered it to the Kits launching ramp and there put it in the water for the day's trip. We fished for salmon, water-skied, and cruised all around the Howe Sound. And we drank a lot of beer. It was a great time and Peter was a super companion, affable, with a great sense of humour.

Though Peter bought the original rig for one thousand dollars, just about everything after that to do with boating came out of my pocket. I did all the upkeep. I summarized and winterized the boat and motor each year, bought new canvas top and seats when needed, scraped the bottom of barnacles, bought a new trailer, and mostly supplied the gas and beer. Oh and Lynda usually supplied the sandwiches. It is with all this contribution in mind that I started to refer to it as 'our boat'. Had I not been involved, the boat would never have left the backyard. All in all, once I accepted the whole concept, Pete's fine company was a worthwhile trade off.

The prime destination for most of our boat trips was Gibson's Landing on the Sunshine Coast of BC. Lynda's family has held vacation property there for many years, and Peter and I would end up there at the end of a day's fishing and often stay the night. It was about an hour and a half full run from Vancouver.

Later, Lynda's aunt gave her and Peter the exclusive use of the main floor of the beach house. This was fantastic: a house on the water with one of the most gorgeous views in the world, looking east to Keats Island and southwest through the Gibson's Gap towards the Gulf Islands and Vancouver Island beyond. This was and still is a paradise as far as I am concerned, and we spent lots of family weeks and weekends up there. The children played as little ones, and later, in some cases came of age on those very beaches.

As Peter became a husband, then a father, and a father, and a father again, his availability for boating decreased so at the end of one summer, when the boat engine died, we gave up that boat. I immediately purchased another one. This was the *Knightsbridge* a sleek twenty-six foot cabin cruiser. It had two twin births, a galley and a walk-in head. I loved it.

The Knightsbridge.

By now the Children were all doing their own things and had no interest in tripping along with the old folks so Lynda and I toured extensively for the next ten years.

I kept the boat in the water all summer long from Easter to Thanksgiving. Lynda often picked me up by car from work on a Friday night, and we drove to the marina, loaded up and off we went. Sometimes we just cruised over to Bowen Island, a couple of miles from Vancouver but a million miles from city cares. There is something amazingly therapeutic about waking up in a marina and sharing breakfast with a passing Mallard. I love those ducks.

87. Dad's failing health.

Dad finally retired and in spite of worsening health problems, always had time to train a new generation of card sharks – his Great Grandchildren.

Sixtieth wedding anniversary

During their retirement years, Mum and Dad travelled. A lot. Visiting me in Canada thirteen times, where they had another loving family almost as large as the one at home. Dad, through his connections with his old Regiment had been awarded some pensions and allowances that he, in his retirement years accepted. The result was that they were never as well off as they were in their old age. They spent time in Mum's hometown of Cobh, rekindling the Irish connection with their nieces and nephews. They travelled to Holland and visited with Margaret, Mum's dear sister Nancy's eldest daughter and her family.

With the piling up of maladies, how he kept going we do not know. He became a veritable medical marvel. On top of a weak heart, he had crippling and painful arthritis in his shoulders and knees. He developed a form of cancer (lymphoma) in 1986, plus he suffered a series of mini-strokes.

I have to thank Mum and all my sisters for their tender loving care, and in particular, Ellen 'the matron', and her daughter Michelle without whose attention we would have been deprived of several precious years with Dad. Of this, I am certain.

But time was running out for Dad. He had been poked, prodded; nuked and sliced so many times he was getting very tired. That great loving heart of his was finding it harder and harder to fight back the never-ending assaults on his body. He never complained. The lumps got bigger and came back quicker. He never complained. In his view, there was always someone worse off than he.

In the summer of 2000, it became apparent to Dad that his condition was not responding to treatment and his general health ruled out a surgical option. He knew and in our hearts we knew that he might not beat this one. At Dad's request, we moved him to St. Catherine's Hospice in Crawley, where of all things he immediately suffered a massive stroke from which he succumbed and died. Our last conversation there was about how we owed each other everything and therefore absolutely nothing. I took some comfort in the fact that he beat the cancer. I truly believe that he did in fact fulfill his self-imposed obligation to leave the world in general, and Cuckfield in particular, a better place for him having lived in it. The Youth Club was his legacy, or more accurately the hundreds of children who passed through it. A testament to this was the high street full of people and the packed church with full military honours for his funeral. One of the Legionnaires was Dick Baird who was my Scoutmaster for the short period of time I spent before being thrown out.

At the reception he leaned over to me and said, "You know what Ron?"

"What?" says I.

"You were a little bugger when you were a boy" pause. "And you know what else? So was your Dad".

I was never more proud.

He leaves his descendants with one hell of a challenge – theirs to accept.

88. Mum is a lost soul.

With the passing of Dad, it became clear that he, and Ellen to a degree, had been covering for Mum's dilapidation. She was not quite with it and incapable of independent living. When Ellen and Roy suddenly upped and left for Spain with their entire family, accommodation had to be found for Mum. She went into an assisted living apartment but never settled and if it were not for her friendship with a fellow 'in-mate', Charles, she would not have lasted there anytime at all. As Mum's mental capacity deteriorated, she was moved into a care home. She hated it. The fact is, I think Mum was suffering from some form of dementia from way back before Dad died, and never was able to adjust to life without him.

In spite of the fact she never had much of an opportunity to flex her intellectual muscle, Mum had a good life. It is though, a great sadness to me that this super woman died so unhappy. She led her life, for her family, in the shadow of her always-popular husband. 'Behind every great man . . .'

89. Retirement.

Retirement kind of snuck up on me. In the last few years at The RGROUP I was doing lots of production and installation of sales environments for massive Real Estate developments. When I left the company I simply formed my own company KnightsBridge Graphic Services, contacted some small design companies and became their production arm. It worked great. I made more money in those last five years then in any previous five. This once again proves the adage that while you can make a good living working for someone else you can only make money working for yourself.

My friend John Linnell and I had played music together for many years, but now being both in some sort of retirement mode allowed us some time to play regularly. We became a 'dynamic duo' playing 50s and 60s pop music in pubs, Legions, and at private parties. We were not at all bad but more importantly we had fun.

This all came to a shuddering halt when I got the big 'C' in 2008. One of the by-products of this illness was the destruction of my self-confidence. For nearly two years I played no music, no Bridge and became a quieter person. I actually became quite a nice chap during this period, too intimidated to be intimidating. Neither lasted.

90. Sheila joins the cosmos.

I might as well address the third great loss in my immediate family, the all too early demise of Sheila.

She and I were great pals throughout her life. We are very alike in many and maybe not particularly admirable ways. A distinct and some might say twisted sense of humour followed her everywhere and stayed to the end. She took no prisoners, and to use a Hockey analogy, if you went into a corner with her you better keep your head up. But she was incomparable in so many other ways. Vibrant, flamboyant, and artistic, she had flair, panache, and chutzpah. What a force.

From the placid days of playing sweethearts as little children, through her sometimes-awkward adolescence, into adulthood and a full life, we stayed close. She tolerated my Catholic guilt laden need to pass moral judgment on her activities and listened to my lectures and admonishments with surprising equanimity.

Her second marriage to Henry was a great if tumultuous success. They had one lovely daughter together; Lucy, and Henry would 'discover' another one, Catherine.

Sheila, I miss you greatly.

91. Epilogue.

The following years have flown by. We have lived, loved, and been happy. We have survived three amazing children all of whose company I would trade for *none* other. They are my closest friends.

We have a wonderful daughter-in-law Cathy, who has presented us with two adorable grandchildren to spoil. This is truly icing on our life's cake. We now also look forward to being part of Susie and Ashley's lives.

We have the Carlow's, Lou, Al, Don & Sue, my Squirrely Guy & Christine, Roberta, my bridge buddies – Peter, Lloyd and Bev, and my mentors JC and John. Bless 'em all.

Emigration is no game for pussies. I try to give the benefit of the doubt to newcomers, as I do have some idea what it means to be far from everything that you have grown to consider safe and comfortable. I survived but when I am asked would I do it again, the answer is complex. I would not trade what I have for anything else in the world though trade-offs are part of the picture. I miss the time I did not spend with my Mum, Dad and sisters. I miss the Sussex countryside, as they say 'you can take the boy out of the country but you can't take the country out of the boy'. I will always be a country boy, somewhat lost in a city.

Village life with all of its busybody detractions is a wonderful community existence. To walk through the town and nod to everyone you meet is cherishing.

Not that all are your friends but they are your neighbours and you harbour some responsibility to and from them. BC is vast and magnificent and I do love to get out for a drive to experience it. The difference between it and Sussex is there are an infinite variety of routes that can be taken on a Sunday afternoon drive through the English hills and dales, whereas here you only have one road north, south or east and west. To see something quite different needs a much longer trip.

After my rocky start in Canada in which I moved seventeen times in the first few years, Lyn and I have lived at 4034 for the past thirty-six. I have had just three jobs in that time each lasting for about ten years. For the most part, I truly loved my work and the people I met doing it, many of whom are close friends to this day.

We have travelled both with or without our children to: Honolulu, Maui, Ibiza, Laguna, San Francisco, Disneyland, Puerto Vallarta, Phoenix, The Grande Canyon, France, Spain, Greece, Italy, Ireland as well as of course many trips to England.

I survived a run in with cancer in 2008 and some nasty following complications. All a very frightening and a dramatic reminder of one's mortality. But as is said, what don't kill yer makes you stronger.

Now retired and comfortable, our time is our own to share with each other, our family and friends. I love my movie work, walking my dog and the game of Bridge that I still play once a month with my old McKim colleagues of some forty years, plus Bev and I have partnered up to play competition (Duplicate) Bridge on a weekly bases.

I have tried here to be historically accurate while adding my own slant on events. I have deliberately left personal details about my children out of this book – I think having me as a father has sufficiently beaten up on their psyche without adding to it here.

I believe that wisdom is the carefully considered combination of knowledge and experience – I will continually strive for this.

My grandfather was an only son. He had two sons only one of whom produced a son. I have two fine boys neither of whom has produced a male heir.

It is possible that the Pelham-Knight dynasty will end with them. According to the famous historical document called *The Domesday Book*, our linage began in England with the birth, to a Norman nobleman from Poitiers in France, of a son to be named John Pelham-Knight. He became the Constable of Pevensey Castle, situated on the south coast near Hastings in Sussex.

Over the years, I have both enjoyed and come to terms with all these interesting things. You may make of them what you will.

As for Lynda and I, in health, our future is bright. We want to continue to travel while we can, meet new people and contribute to the world around us as best we can. I will stay in touch with politics and work at them from time to time as the urge grabs me. I doubt I will ever embrace unions but I must admit to some growing frustration at the burgeoning gap between Joe Average and the wealthy which may if unimpaired move me a bit towards the centre – Right? And Finnegan's goat will salute the Union Jack.

So, did two Rons make a Knight?

Well he did his damndest and I did my best,

from the Wield of Sussex o'er the Rockies' crest.

He was the last of his kind and stood to the test,

but following a legend was no easy quest.

KNIGHTS BRIDGE

© 2013 Knightsbridge Graphic Services Inc

r_knight@shaw.ca

Made in the USA
San Bernardino, CA
24 November 2013